FIGHTER PILOT

FIGHTER PILOT

A Personal Record of the Campaign in France 1939–1940

Wing Commander Paul Richey DFC & BAR

CHEVALIER DE LA LÉGION D'HONNEUR

OFFICER OF THE ORDER OF THE CROWN OF BELGIUM

FRENCH CROIX DE GUERRE WITH PALM

BELGIAN CROIX DE GUERRE WITH PALM

ROYAL HUMANE SOCIETY'S BRONZE MEDAL FOR

SAVING LIFE FROM DROWNING.

Edited by Diana Richey

CASSELL

Cassell
Wellington House, 125 Strand, London WC2R 0BB

First published by B. T. Batsford Ltd 1941
Revised editions 1955, 1969, 1980, 1990
This edition, reset and further revised, 2001
First Cassell Military Paperbacks edition 2002
Reprinted 2003, 2004

British Library Cataloguing-in-Publication Data
A catalogue record for this book is available from the British Library

ISBN 0-304-36339-1

Designed by Gywn Lewis

Printed and bound in Great Britain by
Cox & Wyman, Reading, Berks.

ACKNOWLEDGEMENTS

The photographs that enlarge and supplement this edition were carefully selected by Paul Richey from unpublished contemporary photographs in the Établissements Cinématographique des Armées, Fort d'Ivry, France; the Bundesarchiv, Koblenz, Germany; the Imperial War Museum, London, as well as from some of his friends' collections and his own.

In thanking most warmly the individuals and organizations concerned, I would also like to express my appreciation to *Fighter Pilot*'s posthumous publishers: Leo Cooper (1990), the sensitive publisher who understood; and Angus MacKinnon of Cassell & Co for his painstaking production of this special edition to celebrate the sixtieth anniversary of the first publication of *Fighter Pilot*.

Diana Richey

'Horatio, I am dead;
Thou livest; report me and my cause aright'

HAMLET, *Act V Scene ii*

CONTENTS

PREFACE

Fighter Pilot started life as a personal journal kept by Paul Richey from the outbreak of war, when he went to France with Number One (Fighter) Squadron in September 1939. After he returned to England in June 1940, Paul was asked by Charles Fry of the publishers B. T. Batsford Ltd if he could see the journal. Having read it, he insisted that Paul should finish it for publication. It was to prove a wise decision. In his preface to that first edition, Charles Fry wrote:

'The author of this book is a Squadron-Leader in the RAF now once again on active service at a Fighter Station in England. His narrative took form from a series of daily diary notes recorded throughout the French campaign, which was 'written up' periodically, when time allowed, in a fat copybook... This manuscript totals over 100,000 words, but contains much material of a personal nature that he has naturally not wished to appear in print... From 10 May onwards, however, the narrative is printed almost exactly as it was written - which was not, it may perhaps be stressed, with any idea of publication in mind. To preserve its first-hand quality as a 'personal record', both he and the publishers have thought it better that little further polishing or embellishment should be attempted.'

The book was received with extraordinary popular and critical acclaim, having caught the mood of a public now aware of the crucial importance of maintaining British air superiority. All the reviews were wildly enthusiastic, but *The Listener* of 16 October 1941 went to the heart of the matter: 'The thrills of aerial combat cannot be put over at second hand. The only hope was that there would be some pilot sufficiently articulate to tell us the real story in the first person. Everybody should read this book... to fill out Mr. Churchill's famous phrase in the mind, to know the real thing, hot from the press of action.'

Charles Fry later published an account of his working with Paul Richey in the 1943 history of his publishing house (*1843-1943 A Batsford Century*, edited by Hector Bolitho) from which this is an extract:

'The best books to come out about the war in the air have been written by the pilots themselves. The first of them to make any stir was Paul Richey's *Fighter Pilot*, which we published anonymously. Paul was not an easy author to deal with, because he was too much interested in the immediate moment and what he would do in the war next day... But he had written a remarkable manuscript, in the heat of the weeks of battle. It was a frank and startling statement of the fighter pilot's mind. The manuscript came into my hands when I met Paul again... after the Battle of France... I had to cajole him from his fighter station near London... He would meet enemy aircraft in combat during the day and hurry up to London to work on his proofs at night. I came across the restless spirit of the fighter pilot for the first time and I came also, in him, to realize the selfless gallantry and sense of adventure that impelled those men. He would work for an hour and then demur, 'Let's go to a nightclub!' So, night after night, a chapter would be taken off to the Nuthouse or some other such smoky joint, and there, with bottles at our elbows and a band blaring into the crowded room, we would correct a few more pages for the printer.

'*Fighter Pilot* sold 75,000 copies as quickly as we could produce them. We could have sold twice as many if it were not for paper restrictions. *Fighter Pilot* began a new phase of publishing for us. It was what the Americans call a war documentary.'

Under the rigid censorship restrictions in force in 1941, *Fighter Pilot* was subjected to a series of exhaustive checks. First, content verification and clearance from Paul Richey's commanding officer, station commander, group commander, Fighter Command and the Air Ministry. Air Commodore Harald Peake, RAF Director of Public Relations at the time, was pivotal in clearing the book through the final stages of this process. The book could not be faulted on fact and detail.

Between 10 and 19 May 1940, with the Squadron confronted by the full might of Hitler's 'Blitzkrieg', Paul Richey was shot down in combat three times, made two parachute escapes from disabled aircraft and was finally shot down in combat and critically wounded. In 1941, on offensive sweeps over enemy-occupied France, he was shot down again and rescued from the Channel, twice escaped by parachute, and made three forced landings in damaged and burning aircraft. His final confirmed score was eleven enemy aircraft destroyed and nine probably destroyed. He then went on to meet the Japanese in Burma and to end the war in the tragic ruins of a defeated Germany.

In his 'Appreciation' of *Fighter Pilot* in the *Illustrated London News*, 27 September 1941, Sir John Squire wrote:

'The author, although young, is in that long and august succession of men of action who could think clearly and express themselves clearly, which included commanders like Xenophon, Caesar and the Duke of Wellington, and many of humbler rank… The whole book is so decent and modest and brave and gay that it seems almost vulgar to mention the fact.'

Diana Richey
SYDNEY, DECEMBER 2000

THE AUTHOR

'. . . one of the outstanding men of Fighter Command.'

Group Captain Lord Leonard Cheshire VC OM DSO DFC

Paul Richey was born in London in 1916 when his father, Lieutenant-Colonel George Richey CMG DSO and Bar, was in the trenches in France. His mother was Australian. Educated at the Institut Fisher, Switzerland, and at Downside in England, most of his youth was spent with his family in Albania, Switzerland and France.

Commissioned in the Royal Air Force in May 1937, he trained as a fighter pilot on Hawker Furies and in March 1939 was posted to No.1 Squadron, then converting from Furies to Hurricane Is at Tangmere, Sussex. Severely wounded during the Battle of France, he spent his convalescence as a fighter operations sector controller at Middle Wallop during the Battle of Britain, then became a fighter operations instructor at No.55 Operational Training Unit, Aston Down, Gloucestershire on Hurricane IIs. In March 1941 he joined No.609 Squadron on Spitfire VBs at Biggin Hill, Kent, as senior flight commander. There followed six months of intensive operations on offensive sweeps over France, after which he took command of No.74 Squadron, also on Spitfire VBs. Head-hunted by Air Chief Marshal Sir Sholto Douglas, he was appointed Squadron Leader Tactics at Headquarters Fighter Command. In May 1942 he took command of No.609 Squadron on Typhoon Is at Duxford, Cambridgeshire, later taking them to Biggin Hill to deal with German low-level fighter-bomber raids on South Coast towns.

In November 1942 he was sent as a wing commander to the India-Burma theatre to revise RAF fighter tactics against the Japanese, and later commanded No.165 Fighter Wing at Comilla and in the Arakan, and No.189 Fighter Wing at Imphal, both on Hurricane IVs.

Invalided home in March 1944, in November he was sent to Brussels as A3 (Operations) to the Supreme Headquarters Allied Expeditionary Forces mission to Belgium. In March 1945 he became a Wing Commander Operations in the War Room of the Headquarters, 2nd Tactical Air Force, Brussels, moving with it to Germany in April 1945, where he spent a year on special duties. In 1948 he joined No.601 (County of London) Squadron as senior flight commander at Hendon, Middlesex, on Spitfire XVIs. He was in command of this unit when it converted to Vampire V jets at North Weald, Essex, in 1949 and commanded it until 1952.

He was three times married with five children.

Dedicated European of wide cultural interests, superb athlete, ocean-racing sailor, deep sea diver, post-war oil executive, trouble-shooting air correspondent, he was writing a history of Anglo–French relations culminating in the air battle of France 1940, when he died on 23 February 1989. The book proclaims the man.

D. R.

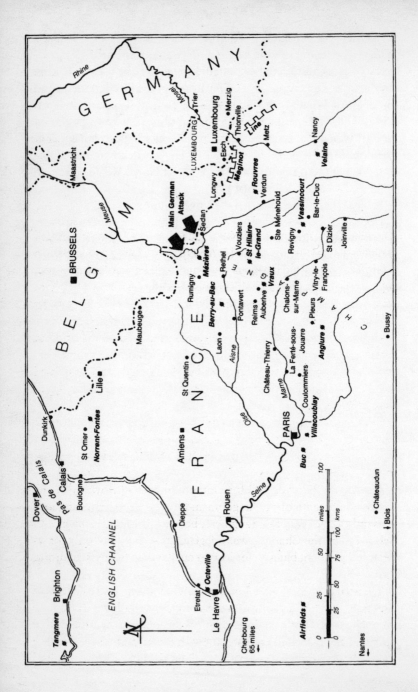

I

FIGHTER COMMAND

I caught my first glimpse of No 1 Squadron in 1937 on a brilliant summer's day at the annual RAF Display at Hendon. Above a thrilled crowd a flight of four silver-and-red Hawker Furies looped, rolled and stall-turned in faultless unison. They were flown by Flight Lieutenant Teddy Donaldson and Flying Officers Top Boxer, Johnny Walker and Prosser Hanks – 1 Squadron's formation aerobatic team. They were to go on to the international aerobatic competition at Zurich, where they astonished the Swiss, Italians, French and Germans by taking off in such dirty weather that the other teams refused to fly and performing their normal aerobatic routine with the cloud-base at 200 feet. They won.

Driving back that evening to my RAF flying training school in Lincolnshire, I was impatient for the day when I would be a member of a fighter squadron. Eighteen months later I was posted to 1 Squadron at Tangmere.

During the two years before my posting I had flown over the length and breadth of our kingdom and had come to know and love it as only a pilot can. But Tangmere, between the South Downs and Selsey Bill on the Channel, was a legendary station, not only for its beautiful position, but also for its two outstanding fighter squadrons, 1 and 43.

On arrival at Tangmere I was somewhat alarmed to hear about the 'flap' that had swept through the fighter squadrons during the Munich crisis a few months earlier. All the 1 Squadron officers had spent a hectic week in the hangars with the aircraftsmen spraying camouflage paint on the brilliant silver aircraft. The troops had belted ammunition day and night. And the CO of 1 Squadron (which was equipped with obsolete Hawker Fury biplanes carrying two slow-firing machine-guns and capable of a top speed of 220 mph) had announced to his startled pilots: 'Gentlemen, our aircraft are too slow to catch the German bombers: we must ram them.'

Fortunately for the RAF, England and the world, Mr Chamberlain managed to stave off war for a year. That vital year gave the RAF time to re-equip the regular fighter squadrons with Hurricanes and Spitfires armed with eight rapid-firing machine-guns and capable of an average top speed of 350 mph.

Re-equipment at Tangmere was completed early in 1939. Half the pilots of each squadron now had to be permanently available on the station in case of a German attack. Gone were the carefree days, when we would plunge into the cool blue sea at West Wittering and lie on the warm sand in the sun, or skim over the waters of Chichester Harbour in the squadron's sailing dinghy, or drive down to the 'Old Ship' at Bosham in the evening with the breeze whipping our hair and 'knock it back' under the oak rafters. Our days were now spent in our Hurricanes at air drill, air firing, practice battle formations and attacks, dogfighting – and operating under ground control with the new super-secret RDF (later called Radar).

The standard of flying in 1 Squadron was red hot. Johnny Walker and Prosser Hanks, members of the 1937 aerobatic team, were still with the Squadron. Johnny was flight commander of 'A' Flight, to which I was posted, and Prosser later took command of 'B' Flight. 1 Squadron was one of the last to convert to the Hurricane, and our first object was to de-bunk it as a rather fearsome aircraft. The Air Ministry had forbidden formation aerobatics to be attempted at all, or individual aerobatics below 5,000 feet. 1 Squadron proceeded to demonstrate that the Hurricane could be easily and safely aerobatted both in formation and below 5,000 feet.

Some of our pilots were killed. One dived down a searchlight beam at night and hit the Downs at 400 miles an hour. And I vividly remember, half an hour before I took a Hurricane up for the first time, seeing a sergeant pilot coming in for a forced landing with a cut engine. He was too slow on the final turn and spun into the ground on the edge of the airfield. I was the first to reach him: he had been flung clear, but blood was running out of his ears and he was dying. However, fatal accidents were a fact of flying life, and 1 Squadron's peace-time average of one per month was considered normal.

During the annual RAF air exercises in midsummer a foreign air force was allowed to fly over England for the first time: French bombers 'attacked' London. We intercepted them with the aid of RDF at 14,000 feet in bright sunshine off the south coast. How gay they looked with their red, white and light blue markings! But how pathetically out-of-date. Later that day Johnny Walker and I intercepted three RAF Blenheims low over the Downs under a violent thunderstorm. They looked grim and businesslike, with mock German crosses on their wings . . .

Shortly after the Exercises we were visited by Squadron Leader Coop, British assistant air attaché in Berlin. He gave us a lecture on the *Luftwaffe*. We were staggered by the number of superbly equipped German bomber and fighter squadrons. These figures rammed home what a narrow escape England had had at the time of Munich, and as that glorious last summer of 1939 rolled on it became clear that it was no longer a question of whether there would be a war, but merely when it would come.

In August we were told we would soon be leaving for France. Shortly afterwards one of our hangars was stacked with the transport and mobile equipment we would take with us. We heard that several RAF Fairey Battle squadrons had already left and we would be off any moment. And we also heard that Air Marshal 'Stuffy' Dowding, Commander-in-Chief of Fighter Command, was kicking up a stink with the Air Ministry: Dowding strongly objected to surrendering the four fighter squadrons earmarked to go to France with the British Expeditionary Force – 1, 73, 85 and 87. He had even paid us the compliment of stating that he would not hold himself responsible for the defence of London if we were sent abroad.

On 1 September Hitler invaded Poland. On Sunday morning, 3 September, all our officers gathered in the mess at eleven-fifteen to hear Mr Chamberlain's broadcast to the nation. It was with heavy hearts and grave faces that we heard the sad voice of that man of peace say: 'This country is at war with Germany . . . We and France are today, in fulfilment of our obligations, going to the aid of Poland, who is so bravely resisting this wicked attack on her people . . . Now may God bless you all. May He defend the right. It is the evil things that we shall be fighting against: brute force, bad faith, injustice, oppression and persecution. Against them I am certain that right will prevail.'

II
BRITISH EXPEDITIONARY FORCE AIR COMPONENT

No 1 Squadron was called to Readiness at dusk on the first night of war. At stand-by in our blacked-out crewroom we sat around talking fitfully or just drowsed. I thoughtfully considered two of the Squadron's World War I trophies hanging in the gloom near the ceiling: the fins of a Pfalz and a Fokker, both bearing the sinister German black cross.

An intelligence report came in: 'Heavy concentration of German bombers crossing the Dutch frontier.' A few minutes later Johnny, Sergeant Soper and I were scrambled and we roared off one by one down the flare-path. Johnny went first, I followed. After I had cleared the airfield hedge, got my wheels up and checked my instruments, I looked for Johnny's amber formation light, spotted it and climbed after him. Soon I was tucked in beside him, with Soper on the other side, and we climbed up to our patrol height of 20,000 feet and opened out into battle formation.

As we droned up and down between Brighton and Portsmouth we could see the coastline clearly below us under the bright full moon. But the whole country was in darkness. Not a single light showed, in sharp contrast to our previous night flights, with Southampton, Portsmouth, Brighton and every town and village along the coast lit up like Christmas trees.

After an hour on patrol without sighting a German aircraft we were recalled by radio and returned. Another section had been sent off, in spite of ground mist that threatened to blot out the airfield.

Soon after landing we were warned to expect seven RAF Whitley heavy bombers which would land at dawn on their return (it was hoped) from bombing the Ruhr. Only two turned up. We watched them trying to find the airfield in the ground mist and fired off Verey lights to help them. They got down all right and we clustered round them. I noticed a bunch of paper sticking to the tail-wheel of a Whitley and grabbed a handful of it. It was a selection of messages from the British Government to the German people, in German. So that was all they had dropped! The Phoney War was on.

That first week of war at Tangmere was tense. There was no more news of our impending departure for France and our time was spent standing-by our Hurricanes and scrambling at each alarm. We expected to be bombed at any moment, but no bombers came and the tension gave way to a feeling of unreality. It was difficult to realize that we were really at war, and that men were dying in thousands on the Polish frontier while all was peaceful here. The sun shone just the same, the old windmill on the hill looked just the same, the fields and woods and country lanes were just the same. But we were stalked by a feeling of melancholy that resolved into the fact: we are at war. At last, on 7 September, we were ordered to France.

At nine-thirty on the morning of Friday, 8 September, I was snatching a few minutes' sleep in my room when my batman came in and said: 'Colonel Richey to see you, Sir' and in walked my father. I was very glad to see him and we sat and talked of nothing in particular. At ten-thirty my batman dashed in again: 'No 1 Squadron called to Readiness, Sir!' I embraced my father and hurried down to the airfield with the other pilots. We were soon grouped beside our Hurricanes. As they were started up one by one, Leak Crusoe took a photograph of the whole team. We ripped the Squadron badges from our overalls (by order) and I gave mine to a fitter to take to my father, who was leaning over the airfield fence watching us. We jumped into our cockpits, and as I taxied past I waved him goodbye. We knew and understood each other's thoughts. There was no time, or inclination, for more.

We took off in sections of three, joining up, after a brief individual beat-up, into flights of six in sections-astern, then went into aircraft-line-astern. Down to Beachy Head for a last look at the cliffs of England, then we turned out across the sea. As we did so Peter Townsend's voice came over the R/T from Tangmere: 'Goodbye and good luck from 43 Squadron!'

There was not a cloud in the sky, scarcely a breath of wind on the sea, and the heat in the cockpits was almost unbearable, as we had on all our gear – full uniform, overalls, web equipment, revolver, gas mask slung, and Mae West. Only the almost complete absence of shipping in the Channel brought home to us the fact that there must be a war on somewhere. After about thirty minutes Dieppe appeared through the heat haze and we turned down the coast towards Le Havre.

Our airfield at Havre lay north-west of the town on the edge of 400-foot cliffs. It was new and spacious, with an unfinished hangar on one side. On the other side, surrounded by trees, was a long, low building that turned out to be a convent that had been commandeered to billet us. The Squadron closed in, broke up into flights of six, then sections of three and, after appropriately saluting the town, came in to land individually. We taxied in to a welcome from our troops: No 1 Squadron had arrived in France, the first of the British fighter squadrons to do so.

The evening was spent in the town – the *Guillaume Tell*, the *Normandie*, the *Grosse Tonne* and *La Lune* following each other in rapid succession. *La Lune*, I may add, was a brothel, but its main attraction for us was that its drinking amenities were untrammelled by such trifling considerations as time. The town was full of Americans trying to escape from the war zone to the States, and a very cheery lot they were. They were full of admiration for our formation flying; they were full of grog too, and a good time was had by all.

The next day found us sober and very very sorry. Our squadron leader, Bull Halahan, smartly rid us of our hangovers – the next three hours were spent digging a trench in the convent orchard for use in the event of a raid. The sun beat down on our sweating bodies and reeling heads and the alcohol literally poured out of us. At eleven we stopped work – fortunately, as none of us was capable of continuing. Buckets of cold water from the pump pulled us round a little – and then over to the aircraft for a squadron formation.

Soon we were in our cockpits, most of us in shirt-sleeves in the heat. Engine after engine burst into life and was run up by its pilot. The Bull's order came clearly over the R/T: 'Come on, we're off! We're off!' He taxied past, followed by Hilly Brown and Leslie Clisby, who formed his section of three. Then came Johnny Walker, Pussy

Palmer and Sergeant Soper, the Red Section of 'A' Flight, followed by Prosser Hanks, myself and Stratton, the Yellow Section. Next came 'B' Flight – Leak Crusoe, Boy Mould, Sergeant Berry (Blue Section), and Billy Drake, Sergeant Clowes and Sergeant Albonico (Green Section).

The fifteen Hurricanes move forward together with a deep roar, slowly at first, then gathering speed. Tails come up, and controls get more 'feel'. Bump-bump-bump. Almost off. A bit frightening, this take-off. We fly! No . . . down we come again. Bump . . . Blast! Must have been a down-draught . . . Hold it! We're off now – straight over the cliff edge 400 feet above the sea. I see Prosser shut his eyes in mock terror. It *is* an odd feeling. As usual, I start to talk to myself. Wheels up. Keep in. Stick between knees. Come on, bloody wheels! Dropping behind a bit. Open your throttle! More! Wide! Ah, there are the two pretty red lights: the wheels are locked up. Now get in closer, for God's sake! The Bull's giving it too much throttle, blast him! Anyway – I'm tucked in now. That's fine.

'Sections astern – Sections astern – Go!' over the R/T from the Bull. Back drops my section of three, a little left and underneath. There we are. Don't waffle, Pussy, or I'll chew up your tail! Up we climb. Phew, it's hot! But I'll bet it looks nice. Hope so anyway.

Out we go over the sea. Flying south I think. Yes, there's the far side of the Seine. 'Turning right – turning right a fraction!' from the Bull. Round and out to sea again. Keep below Prosser in the turn – that's right. Hell, the sun's bloody bright! I can't see Prosser's wing when he's above me in the turn. Don't hit him! Watch his tailplane! The Bull again: 'Coming out – coming out!' We straighten. Ah, that's better – I can see now. And the Bull once more: 'For Number 5 Attack – Deploy – Go! Sections-line-astern – Go! Number 5 Attack – Go!'

Open out a bit. There goes Johnny. Now Pussy. Soper. Prosser next. Now me. Down I go. Watch 'B' Flight and synchronize with them. Pull up now. Fire! Break away quickly. Roll right over and down to the right. Rejoin. Where's Prosser got to? Can't see a bloody thing. Ah, there he is, up there. Full throttle! Up – up – cut the corner. Here we come behind him. Throttle back or you'll pass him. And there we are again, back in line-astern.

Prosser's waggling his wings. That means form Vic. 'Re-form! – Re-form!' from the Bull. 'Turning right now!' Towards Havre? Yes, there it is dead ahead. 'Sections-echelon-starboard – Go!' Right goes my section. Up. Left. Keep in! There, that's nice, really nice. The whole squadron is now in Vics of three aircraft and the five Vics are echeloned to starboard. Now, fingers out please 1 Squadron. Hope we don't overshoot. No, here we go. 'Peel off – peel off – Go!' says the Bull. His section banks left in formation beyond the vertical and disappears below. Johnny's section follows. Don't watch them – keep your eyes glued to Prosser. Here goes my section now. Down, down we dive in tight Vic, turning slightly left. Keep in – tucked right in! Stratton is OK the other side of Prosser. Right a bit. The controls are bloody stiff – must be doing a good 400. Flattening out now. Don't waffle! There goes the harbour. Buildings flashing by. We're nice and low. Keep in! Hold it! Pulling up now – up – over the rise – over the airfield now. *Down* we go again – just to make the Frogs lie down. Up over the trees – just! Round and back again. Good fun, this. Bet they're enjoying the show down there. I am! Here we go again, skimming the grass and heading straight for the trees. Pull up – up come our noses and we just clear them. Prosser's waving his hand. Break away! There goes Stratton's belly – away we go, nicely timed, in a Prince of Wales, and I'm on my own.

What now? God, I feel ill! Let's give the old girl a last shake-up. What about an upward roll? Good idea – but watch the others – the air's full of flying bodies! Let's climb. Down in that clear space. Need some speed for this. 300-350-360. That's enough. Adjust the tailwheel. Now back with the stick. Gently up – up – a touch harder now. Horizon gone – look out along the wing. Wait till she's vertical – now look up. Stick central, now over to the right of the cockpit. Round she goes. Stop. Back with the stick. Look back. There's the horizon, upside down – stick forward – now over to the left – and out we roll. Not bad. Oh my God, I'm going to be sick . . .

Better land. Throttle right back. Slow down to 160 mph. Wheels down. Now flaps. Turn in now. Open the hood. Hold speed at 90. Tailwheel right back. Over the boundary. Hold off a fraction. Sink, sink – right back now with the stick. Bump, rumble, rumble, rumble – fine. No brakes – plenty of room. Tiny bit heavy that one. Not quite right. Oh well. Taxi in – run the petrol out of the carburettor, switch off ignition, brakes off, undo safety and parachute harness and jump out.

I stroll across to join the other pilots. Prosser fixes me with his characteristic dead-pan look.

'You just missed a steeple when we were beating up Havre, Paul,' he says casually.

'Did I?' Equally casual. 'Glad I didn't see it!'

After lunch we watched 73 Squadron arrive from Digby, in Lincolnshire. They were the other squadron in our Wing, No 67, and were to be our partners for the rest of the campaign in France. And a great bunch of chaps they turned out to be.

Then back to the trench-digging. We were determined to finish the rotten chore before tea, regardless of blistered hands and aching backs. By four we were half-dead, but the trench was practically ready. Just as we were heaving the last agonizing spadefuls out the Bull strode up.

'OK boys, you won't be needing that tonight. We leave for Cherbourg in half an hour.'

'Stone the f—ing crows!' Clisby, the Australian, neatly summed up our feelings.

Soon we were in the air again, tired and fed-up. It was still hellish hot. Why's the Bull keeping us in close formation? Ah well – this *is* 1 Squadron. Cherbourg wasn't far, although we couldn't get our hands on any maps and only had hazy ideas of the shape of this region of France. The general opinion was that France turned a corner somewhere hereabouts and continued on down to Spain. However, we found Cherbourg all right – one couldn't miss it – and having blown the paint off a few boats in the harbour – whose occupants seemed to be enjoying things immensely – we came in and landed individually. The airfield looked big enough, but was actually very short, and I finished up in a skid much too near the fence for comfort. Johnny, of all people, overshot and went round again, which made me feel slightly better.

We dispersed the aircraft along a road and were at once surrounded by groups of French sailors. They were conscripts and showed great interest in our Hurricanes, marvelling at their armament and politely incredulous at their performance figures. This was not surprising, for the only aircraft besides small training machines we saw at Cherbourg were Latécoère dive-bombers – high-wing monoplanes with one 640-horsepower Hispano engine (half the horsepower of a

Hurricane), one machine-gun firing through the propeller and another in a rear turret, and carrying two 500 lb bombs, plus the incredible crew of five – pilot, bomb-aimer, gunner, navigator, and engineer! Normal speed was only 80 mph, but right 'off the clock' while dive-bombing. The men who dared dive those ghastly contraptions with that load aboard were worthy of the name.

Refuelling took several hours because of lack of equipment. At last, tired and hungry, we had supper in the officers' mess and went to bed in a barrack hut. Grey sticky sheets washed in sea-water and straw pillows were incidental, and we were soon sleeping gratefully.

Next day we were up at 5 am on a cold, dark, wet Sunday morning. At six my section was off with the light. Cloud-base was at 200 feet generally, and in patches only 50, so after twenty minutes of futile efforts at reaching our patrol line we trailed back and landed. Soon afterwards we saw through the drizzle in the grey half-light the convoy we were there to protect creeping into port, silent and shadowy as ghosts. Later we learnt that it was the grim advance guard of the BEF – the Royal Army Medical Corps hospital and casualty organization.

Later the clouds broke and the day was spent patrolling. I shall always remember that day flying over the beautiful countryside of Normandy, with its fishing villages in washed-out colours, oyster beds, green woods and fields, and its magnificent chateaux with their round pointed towers and spires and formal gardens.

No enemy aircraft were sighted – we hardly expected any – and soon we were being entertained once more by our French hosts. Conversation was somewhat staccato as only a few of us spoke French. But the most difficult part for us was tactfully to correct the fixed notion that the English drank tea with every meal and on every possible occasion. In this we were only partly successful – they thought we were just being polite. We also found that any attempt to save trouble by refusing anything offered was received as a sign of distaste or disapproval; and to do anything for oneself was regarded as an absolute abuse of hospitality.

Next day, Monday, 11 September, we were ordered to return to Havre after lunch. Having drunk to the success of the Allied cause in our hosts' best vintage champagne, we took off at two o'clock.

We were soon back at our own airfield and happy to see the little convent again.

At Havre we were told that our formation beat-up of the town had been a tremendous success. The whole population had been out in the streets. The cafés and bars had emptied in a trice and the place was a mass of waving, gasping humanity. The town was packed with Americans, and Doc Cross, our MO, who had watched the show with the US Consul and several friends, said the expressions of admiration had become positively embarrassing. They had never seen such flying anywhere and so on and so forth. Eventually poor Cross had crept silently away to hide. But 73 had the last laugh: they went into the town that evening and knocked back the free drinks lined up for us!

On our return from Cherbourg there was little doing for a few days. The time was mostly spent booting a ball about, clambering down the cliff to swim, sleeping, writing letters home or avidly reading the few papers that came across from England by air. Our evenings usually kicked off at about six at the *Guillaume Tell*, where we sat over Pernods or vermouths watching the life of the boulevards, and ended in the *Normandie* or elsewhere. We all felt that our first taste of service in France would probably be our last of civilization and peace for a long time and we wanted to make the best of it. I shall always remember Havre with affection – with its fine port, its magnificent view from the hill across to Deauville, its wide boulevards, lively cafés, shops and restaurants – and the church of St Michel, where the old *curé* preached such a moving sermon to the mothers of France, and afterwards heard my confession, giving me the strength and courage to face whatever was to come.*

We left Havre on 29 September. I was flying a reserve machine without parachute (against regulations) or sights, and had to proceed independently, though within sight of the formation, to avoid risk of collision. I took off first and climbed to 8,000 feet in brilliant sunshine and slight haze. Circling slowly, with difficulty I watched the

---

* The Havre we loved no longer exists: in 1944, after the Allied victory in Normandy but while the town was still in German hands, it was reluctantly bombed by heavies of RAF Bomber Command at the British Army's insistence. Owing to a tragic oversight the usual warning to the French underground failed to function, and 8,000 French civilians were killed in the devastation.

Squadron leave the airfield and creep out over the sea. I could hear them chattering away on the R/T but completely lost sight of them over land. Coming down to 5,000 feet I picked them out beating up the town in close formation. They looked like a tiny slug crawling over the ground, although they were five sections in sections-astern. After they passed on I came down in a series of loops, rolls and inversions to say goodbye to Havre in general and to one or two people in particular in the only way possible in a fighter. Then I chased off after the Squadron.

I lost them for twenty minutes and got cold feet as I had no maps, but by going down very low I was able to pick them up in the distance against the sky and watched them like a hawk until I had caught them. They broke up over our new airfield at Norrent-Fontes, near St Omer in the Pas-de-Calais, and I circled to await my turn to land. The place looked a mess. There was only one none-too-long run for taking off and landing, and we were accommodated in tents beside the airfield. The first job we did on landing was latrine-digging. And then it began to rain.

III

ADVANCED AIR STRIKING FORCE

It rained hard for the next two weeks and we did very little flying. The only relief to the monotony was a lecture on what we were supposed to be doing delivered by our air officer commanding, Air Vice-Marshal Blount.

The RAF in France (he told us) was split into two parts.

First, the Air Component of the British Expeditionary Force, comprising four Hurricane fighter squadrons, four Blenheim bomber-reconnaissance squadrons and four Lysander army co-operation squadrons, all based in the Pas-de-Calais. They were to work with the BEF now digging in along the Franco-Belgian frontier and were commanded by Blount himself.

Second, the Advanced Air Striking Force, comprising ten Battle light bomber squadrons based round Reims. They were to work with the French army now holding the Maginot Line along the Franco-German frontier and were commanded by Air Vice-Marshal Playfair.

It was considered that sooner or later (the AOC continued) the Germans would launch an all-out attack on the Western Front and violate the neutrality of Belgium and Luxembourg to break through. In Poland German attacks had been preceded by a thorough air bombardment of all military concentrations, particularly airfields, and this pattern was expected to be repeated.

After the AOC left we fell to discussing his talk. Although the French Air Force was to work with us, we thought we would be taking the brunt of the attack on the British front. Good. We believed our aircraft to be superior to the German machines. Our personnel and training were on the top line, and our morale was more than healthy. We knew the fighting would be tough and continuous and that a lot of us would be killed. Four fighter squadrons to defend the entire British Expeditionary Force! It was absurd. But at least we were not afraid to fight and if necessary to die, and we were confident we would give a good account of ourselves.

A few evenings later we had news from the French front: a Battle squadron had been severely mauled by a bunch of Hun fighters over the Maginot Line. The French fighters had muffed it. The following day the Bull was in his Hurricane headed for Advanced Air Striking Force headquarters at Reims. The news he brought back was exhilarating: he had offered our services to the AASF and they said they would be delighted to have us to look after them. The two AOCs fixed it up between them, Air Ministry agreed, and on 9 October we and 73 were off to the front with our tails up, leaving poor old 85 and 87, who were based at Lille, to their convoy-patrolling over the Channel.

As a matter of fact the BEF made a last effort to stop us! As the Squadron flew in close formation at 1,000 feet over Arras, where General Gort had his headquarters, they were shot up by mistake by British ack-ack gunners with Bofors quick-firers. Luckily the Squadron was moving fast and no one was hit. But I was in charge of the advance party travelling in four French Air Force Wibault T.12 transport aircraft laden with troops, ammunition and essential equipment, and as I was peacefully piloting the leading aircraft (which I must admit did vaguely resemble a Junkers Ju 52 with its three engines) we were suddenly fired on by four British Bofors batteries in concert. But for the skill of our French pilot, *Capitaine* Casanova, who quickly grabbed the controls, we'd have bought it. As it was we collected half a dozen shell holes and had to limp back to Norrent and land. Then we got stuck by bad weather for four days.

Our new airfield was at Vassincourt, near Bar-le-Duc, fifty miles east of Reims. 73 Squadron went to Rouvres, near Verdun, northeast of us. Our airfield was on a hill surrounded by woods. At the foot of the hill passed a canal and a railway line, and on the other side of these lay the little village of Neuville where we were billeted. The Germans had been there twice – in 1870 and 1914 – and the inhabitants bore them no great love. My billet was in an ancient farmhouse, half-timbered, gabled and rambling. My host, of whom more later, worked on the railway as a signalman.

I had my first combat shortly after our arrival, but not quite in the way I had expected. I was sent up alone one afternoon to patrol the airfield at 20,000 feet on the off-chance of intercepting a machine of doubtful nationality we had spotted several times floating about at a great height. On directions given over the R/T by Pete Mathews, sitting in a Hurricane on the ground, I flew west for ten minutes after the suspicious aircraft. The sun was low and I was flying into it. I could see little and found nothing. On the way back I was in a dive at 10,000 feet when I saw what I took to be six Hurricanes about five miles away on my starboard side, flying in the same direction. I went over to have a look and made the mistake of approaching at the same level, thinking they were friendly.

I soon saw the fighters were not Hurricanes. I thought it was unlikely they were Messerschmitts this far over France. While I was studying them the number two aircraft saw me, waggled his wings beside his leader and dived below and towards me. He pulled up, and as he did so I saw the tricolour on his tail. He was a French Morane fighter. Then he opened fire, taking a full deflection shot at me as he climbed. A second Morane attacked.

I had by this time turned steeply left towards the first Frenchman and passed over him. I then dived in a turn to the right, did an Immelmann to the left which took me above a small cloud, stood on my tail, stall-turned and dived in a vertical left-hand spiral at full throttle. One Morane got on my tail, but I reckoned he was out of effective range, and knowing the Hurricane to be less manoeuvrable but faster than the Morane, I straightened out 200 feet above ground and kept a straight course at full throttle. I shook off both the Frogs but was lost: I had taken off in a hurry and had no maps. After circling until it was almost dusk and I had only 20 gallons of petrol left, I returned to a town I had seen, chose a field on top of a hill (for dryness), flew low over it to examine the surface and made two practice approaches with wheels and flaps down. Then I landed on it, up a gentle slope beside some trees, feeling that at least my 20 gallons had been well used.

The town was Joinville. A group of French officers arrived and took charge of me, treated me like a prince, and gave me an excellent dinner in their mess. I learned that one of the French fighters had also force-landed, low on petrol, and had nosed over and broken his prop, so I considered honour satisfied. The pilot had telephoned the police in great excitement and told them to locate the 'German aircraft' that had landed in the district. When informed it was British he just said, with appropriate feeling, *'Merde!'*

Towards the end of the almost too excellent dinner the French pilot was contacted at my request and invited to join us. For a joke he was told that I was wounded. The poor fellow arrived to find me sitting at the table swathed in bandages and surrounded by a crowd of sympathetic *Armée de l'Air* officers. I rose unsteadily as my attacker came in (no wonder after that dinner!). *Sergeant-Chef* Léo Boyer, a tall, fit young Basque, came forward, his frank brown eyes showing deep concern. 'This has gone too far,' I thought, and with a laugh shook his hand with my bandaged one. We sat down and bottles circulated rapidly once more.

Léo and I became firm friends, and he gave me his badge with tears in his eyes: it was the badge of the famous Formation Aerobatic Squadron of Dijon, of which he had been a member. He had been a pilot for eight years. I was told later that he was considered an exceptional pilot by the French Air Force. He confided that he had fired at least 400 bullets and 40 cannon shells at me.

A few weeks afterwards I was sitting next to a French colonel at lunch, and somehow the story came up. The colonel, who commanded the French fighters in our area, told me he had sentenced poor Léo to be confined to his station for a week. 'Not so much for attacking you,' he said with a twinkle, 'as for missing!'

Our first victory was on 30 October 1939 – a gloriously sunny day with no low cloud but quite a lot of high wispy stuff. I was on the airfield by my machine when we heard unfamiliar aircraft engines. After a lot of neck-craning and squinting we saw it – a Dornier 17 immediately above us at some 20,000 feet, travelling west and just visible in the thinner clouds. Like all Luftwaffe aircraft it was light-blue underneath and difficult to spot. The French ack-ack opened up but got nowhere near it.

This was the first Hun we'd seen, and we were wildly excited. Soper and I rushed off in pursuit, but had to watch our take-off and lost him. We saw him again from 3,000 feet, but lost him soon after. Up and up we climbed, turning gently from side to side and straining our eyes to find him. We didn't, and at 25,000 feet, with sights alight and gun-buttons on 'Fire', we cursed like hell and came down after fifteen minutes' search.

Soper was leading me and now realized he was lost. While he circled at 1,000 feet trying to pin-point our position I kept an eye on the sky and suddenly saw a twin-engined aircraft circling a nearby town very high. We climbed 20,000 feet, watching like hawks and keeping directly below him so that he would not spot us. When we were 2,000 feet below we saw his French roundels: a Potez. I flew right up to him to make quite sure and gave him a hell of a fright: he dived away and yanked himself into such a tight turn that vortex plumes streamed from his wing-tips.

Down we went again, and Soper landed on a French airfield to check our position while I circled languidly, bored and angry at losing the Hun. (We heard afterwards that he had turned above a cloud and gone back over our heads.) Soper took off and I scattered the Frenchmen on the ground in a farewell dive, then we flew back to Vassincourt. To add insult to injury a couple more Dorniers flew over the airfield at 15,000 feet while we were having a late lunch at Neuville.

As we went up to the airfield a Hurricane dived across rocking its wings, turned, came back and repeated the performance, obviously highly excited. It was Boy Mould, who had joined the Squadron in June. He had just finished refuelling after a patrol when the same Dornier went over. He took off without waiting for orders, pulled his plug (boost-override), lost the Hun, climbed up to 18,000 feet – and found him. He did an ordinary straight astern attack, firing one longish burst with his sights starting above the Dornier and moving slowly round the fuselage. The Hun caught fire immediately, went into a vertical spiral, and made a whopping hole in the French countryside: it exploded on striking the ground. There were no survivors. The mangled remains of a gun from the aircraft, together with a bullet-pierced oxygen bottle, later adorned our mess as trophies of the first British fighter victory of the war – which was also the first fighter engagement – in France.*

* German records report the loss of this aircraft, which was from 2(F) 123, a day later than that on which it took place.

Five hands was all that remained of the crew of four, but four coffins were given a funeral with military honours at which the Squadron was represented. We were all pleased at our first success, but we were sorry for the poor devils we had killed. Boy got very drunk that night and confided to me, 'I'm bloody sorry I went and looked at the wreck. What gets me down is the thought that *I* did it!'

For three weeks after this incident life was quiet because of heavy rain, and the countryside was flooded. On 23 November the sun set in a blaze of red as the clouds broke, and the following morning was sunny and clear. It was my bad luck to be on duty in the operations room, and there was plenty to think about. The map was covered with 'plots' and we sent patrols off to see what they could do about it. They did quite a lot: we bagged two Dornier 17s and a Heinkel 111; 73 Squadron got three Dorniers. Most of the enemy aircraft crashed in flames, but there were some wounded survivors who had jumped for it.

1 Squadron's first Dornier was intercepted near Metz by the Bull and Hilly Brown. They attacked alternately and continually from astern until the Hun went into a steep spiral and crashed in flames near the lines. I remember talking to the Bull on the R/T and hearing him call out 'Got another one for the Squadron near — !' ' Near where?' I asked, 'Say again!' and he shouted back 'Homburg as in hat!'

The Heinkel was also brought down near Metz, intercepted by Blue Section of 'B' Flight. It was on fire, losing height rapidly, when a bunch of French Moranes came rushing in, all so eager to have a bang that one of them knocked most of Sergeant Clowes' tail off and the pilot had to bale out! Clowes put up a very good show getting his machine back to the airfield, though he had to land at 120 mph to keep control: he overshot and nosed over. I saw him straight after this little effort and, though he was laughing, he was trembling violently and couldn't talk coherently. I had a good look at his aircraft too: one elevator and half the rudder were completely gone. Anyway, the Heinkel came down all right – but to our disgust we were only officially credited with one-third of it: a 73 pilot and the French ack-ack boys also claimed to have shot at it.

A section from 'A' Flight led by Pussy Palmer attacked the other Dornier about twenty miles north of the airfield. Pussy led from dead astern. By the time he had used all his ammunition the rear-gunner and navigator had escaped by parachute and one engine was burning merrily. The Dornier was losing height and seemed to be more or less out of control. Pussy flew alongside the German to make sure the pilot was dead. He saw him slumped in his seat, his head lolling sideways. But suddenly the Dornier throttled back, swerved on to Pussy's tail as he overshot and put exactly thirty-four bullets through his Hurricane. Hearing them rip through, Pussy ducked and pushed the stick forward – thereby saving his life, as a bullet penetrated the locker behind his head and smashed the windscreen. Clouds of white smoke (which proved to be glycol) poured from the engine, which stopped. Pussy undid his straps and prepared to bale out, but the smoke stopped – presumably the glycol was finished – so he strapped up again and crash-landed safely with his undercarriage retracted. Meanwhile, Killy and Soper, numbers 2 and 3 of Pussy's section, attacked the Hun. With both engines now on fire, he crash-landed miraculously more or less in one piece. Killy and Soper circled and saw him wave as they passed low overhead. They returned to Vassincourt and Pussy was picked up by car.

We all admired and respected this German's guts. His machine had at least 500 bullet holes in it – not enough, we thought, considering three Hurricanes had been giving it their full attention. We later heard that to fire his final burst at Pussy he had to leave the pilot's seat (where he had been feigning death) and lock his gun in the fixed position. It was such a good effort that we determined to have him to dine with us in the mess. Easier said than done, for the French authorities were reluctant to part with him. But after a great deal of lobbying we were eventually allowed to send Billy Drake, who spoke French*, to fetch him from Ste Menehould goal, where he had spent the night of his capture. The French had given the poor fellow a thorough grilling, but I don't think they got much out of him. After more wrangling Billy obtained permission to bring him to the Squadron mess, with a gendarme in close attendance – on the strict understanding that he would be delivered to the Citadel at Verdun after dinner.

*Toby Carter, our radar expert, acted as German interpreter.

I was in the *Mairie* hall when the German pilot arrived. He was aged about thirty, of medium height, thick-set and fit, and his clean-shaven face was lean and pleasant. His blue eyes looked directly into mine as he shook my hand and clicked his heels, bowing stiffly from the waist.

'*Unteroffizier* Frankenberger,' he said, and I replied '*Leutnant* Richey.' I led him up the stairs into the mess, which was a long room with a fireplace at one end, a stove and homemade bar at the other, a long refectory table down the centre and various trophies livening -up the walls – a German eagle from a Dornier, a spinner from another, a bashed-up machine-gun from a third, and some humorous drawings by the Squadron artist, Palmer 'Secundus'. But the trophies had been removed on this occasion for reasons of tact.

As we arrived a hush fell on the room and everyone stood up. One by one the officers were introduced, after which an effort was made to make the proceedings less formal. The unfortunate German was feeling uncomfortable under the curious scrutiny of our officers, especially as only a couple of us spoke his language. He was ushered to a chair by the fire, but would not sit down until we did. The wireless was switched on, a foaming silver Squadron tankard was handed to Frankenberger and drinks circulated rapidly. He would not drink unless we did, and stood up instantly when addressed by a standing officer.

But soon he began to relax, and as we plied him with more beer and clinked mugs he became quite cheerful. I think he suspected at first that we were trying to get him tight to ferret information out of him. Anyway, the party warmed up rapidly. He told us his name was Arno, and for the rest of the evening Christian names and nicknames were the only ones used. Still security-conscious, he told us he came from Central Germany, and pulled out his wallet to show us some photographs: himself and some Luftwaffe pals doing a mouth-organ jig in camp; his wife and baby in his little garden; and a postcard of himself in uniform which he signed and presented to the mess. We much admired his fine-quality flying suit and boots. He told us his belt had been confiscated by the French, with an aerial photograph of his house. The Bull volunteered to try and get them back for him.

Arno had been a gliding instructor before the war, then had joined the *Luftwaffe* and had put in 1,000 hours' power-flying. He had volunteered for special reconnaissance duties over enemy territory, and his family knew nothing about it. Seeing a sector map of the German frontier on the mess wall he commented: 'That is nothing! We have detailed maps of all England! All of it!' He examined a silhouette of a Messerschmitt 110 and remarked: 'If I'd been flying *that* I wouldn't be here now.' He declared that the *new* Messerschmitt 109 was superior to the Hurricane, which produced some good-natured shouting on both sides.*

Dinner was punctuated by a rather distressing incident. Hilly Brown was guffawing in his usual whole-hearted way at some aside and unfortunately looking at Arno. 'Why is he laughing at me?' a frowning Arno asked Toby Carter (our RDF man). Embarrassed, Toby replied 'Oh, he's not laughing at you – he's laughing at some stupid joke.' Arno was silent and stared solemnly at his plate. We were startled to see him suddenly rest his head in his hands, hiding his face, as tears fell on his plate. For a ghastly moment there was dead silence; then the Bull and Billy motioned Arno out. We all understood that he must be overwrought after his ordeal in the air and his capture.

He apologized on the stairs and said he was just fed-up with the war. He rejoined us and gradually we cheered him up again.

After dinner the Bull proposed a toast 'To all pilots!' which we happily drank. Pussy, who had just come in, was introduced, and the two pilots who had shot each other down exchanged 'compliments'. The Bull left the party at one o'clock and Arno had to be carted off to Verdun – in spite of his entreaties to be allowed to stay with us or to be sent to England. We were all very merry indeed by this time and followed our guest downstairs to wave him off. It was snowing heavily, and Killy tore off his sweater and handed it to Arno, while Boy insisted that he take his greatcoat. 'You too will be treated well in Germany if you are taken prisoner!' he assured us over and over again in German. When saying *'Auf wiedersehen'* he took each one of us in his arms and kissed us on both cheeks. He was driven off with Billy on one side of him and the inscrutable gendarme on the other, and the quiet village street echoed to three rousing British cheers as the car disappeared in the snow.

*He probably meant the Bf 109E3.

Pussy's combat with Arno had an important sequel that was to save the lives of many RAF fighter pilots. At this time the only armour our fighters carried was a thick cowling over the front petrol tank and a bullet-proof windscreen, while our Battles had thick armour plating behind the pilot – as indeed did the German fighters. After Pussy's lucky escape we decided we should have back armour too, and we asked for it. The Hawker Aircraft Company, maker of the Hurricane, was consulted, but the Air Ministry refused our request because the experts maintained that back armour would affect the Hurricane's centre of gravity and lead to flying difficulties.

So the Bull acted independently. He located a written-off Battle on a nearby bomber airfield and seized the back armour. He then fitted his prize into a Hurricane and carried out flying tests. These were highly satisfactory. The Bull then told Air Ministry of his experiments and sent Hilly over to the Royal Aircraft Establishment at Farnborough to demonstrate the armoured Hurricane to the boffins and experts. Hilly put up a show of aerobatics and manoeuvres that threw everything in the book at them and quite a lot more. The experts were convinced, and back armour was henceforth fitted as standard equipment to RAF fighter aircraft.

IV
ENTENTE CORDIALE

About this time we organized a roster which gave one flight or the other a day off now and then. On such occasions we would escape from our little village and whirl off to Rouvres to see the 73 boys, or press on to Nancy or Metz.

We thought Nancy was a particularly pleasant town – though probably for different reasons. Usually we would lunch together, then bounce round it in good spirits, exciting interest from the crowds, mostly of women, in the busy streets. '*Royale Air Force!*' we could hear them say coquettishly, or '*Il est très joli, ce bleu, n'est-ce pas?*' The boys would generally head straight for the Roxy, but I used to stroll about for a while in the old town, looking at the cathedral, at the Place Stanislas with its beautiful wrought-iron gates, and walking down the seventeenth-century chestnut avenue to the gothic *Basilique de St Evre*.

After wandering about dreaming for a while I found it difficult to wrench myself back from the atmosphere of the *Grand Siècle* at its best as perpetuated in the architecture of Nancy. But the atmosphere of the twentieth century at its worst as typified by the Roxy soon dispelled it. By the time I had bounded up the stairs and was handing my coat to the grinning cloakroom attendant it was already fading fast, to be dissipated entirely as I walked through the doors to the bar. The transition was unpleasant, but the pain was quickly dulled by champagne. The room was low-ceilinged, with a dim, religious light. It had a bar at one end and a dance floor at the other. Round the plush-draped walls were crowded tables and comfortable chairs. The bar was invariably surrounded by a throng of British and French air force officers, French Army officers and 'ladies of the evening' waiting to be given a drink, a good time and anything else one could afford. The dance floor was a wrestling mob, and the air was heavy with smoke, hot rhythm and general clamour. After a drink or two and a few friendly exchanges I would begin to feel it was all quite jolly, and soon would be laughing, chattering and dancing, and no doubt looking as damned silly as I had thought everyone else when I first arrived.

And so it went on, until Johnny would pull himself together with an effort and drag us out an hour or so later than we'd meant to leave. We would be driven away by our heroic driver, Owens (who by this time would have dined at our expense) and would wake tired, cold and rather browned-off bumping down the hill into Neuville. We would then tumble out at the *Mairie* and tramp off in scruff order to our billets to snatch a few hours' sleep before being called in the still cold hours of the morning to get up to the airfield again before dawn.

These expeditions were infrequent, and varied with trips to Paris. The Air Officer Commanding had decreed that all his pilots should have seventy-two hours off in every fifteen days. This was later reduced to sixty hours. Actually it didn't work out as intended for us: the bomber boys had nothing much on operationally except sprinkling occasional pamphlets over the Siegfried Line at night, but the fighter wing had to maintain a full squadron at Readiness or 15 Minutes Available in all weathers. This, combined with the fact that the Bull, with his characteristic foresight, had sent everybody who could be spared on home leave in anticipation of a bust-up in the spring, gave those of us left behind little time off.

The pattern of Paris leave was generally a pleasantly anticipatory train journey (helped along with a whisky bottle); arrival at the *Gare St Lazare*; a taxi along the busy *grands boulevards* to the momentary quiet of a spacious room at the Hotel Crillon; the luxury of a hot bath; then champagne cocktails in the bar before lunch. These before-lunch drinks had a habit of going round and round until three o'clock, when the bar shut. A hiatus would then occur – sometimes filled in by walking round the shops and arcades – until five, when the bars re-opened and the after-effects of 'lunch' could be smartly shot away.

Dinner might be a feature of the evening, but was fairly unlikely.

Possibly we would finish up with a champagne supper in one of our rooms. Or perhaps we would pay a visit to our friend Marjorie – a Canadian dress designer who kept open house for the Squadron and won us all by her generosity, her cheerful tolerance of our rowdy behaviour and her general interest in us. Marjorie was a marvel, and the Bull made her the Squadron's first honorary member. From her flat we would stampede into a taxi and arrive with a roar at the *Boeuf-sur-le-Toit*, where we paid exorbitant sums for the doubtful privilege of sitting in a smoky room drinking more champagne, only vaguely aware of the surrounding company of glamorous females, French Army officers, international pansies, crooks and spies. The pianist Jack Wilson would habitually bang out 'We're goin' ter hang out the washing on the Siegfried Line', first in French, then in English for our benefit. There would be an embarrassed lull while we tried to sing it and pretend to enjoy it. The cafés shut at eleven, so it would be early to bed and late to rise the next morning – but not too late to get well lit up again by lunchtime.

On one such evening in Paris I got more plastered than usual. I can remember dining at Maxim's. I can remember going to George's Bar. I can remember eventually reaching the APNA, the French professional aviators' club. I can even remember dancing the Boomps-a-Daisy with Colonel Rosanoff,* a well-known French test pilot. We drank a toast *'A la victoire!'* and I joyously hurled my empty glass at the wall behind the bar instead of on the floor, scattering shrapnel over the assembly and denting the wall. My apologies were laughed off as they made me sign the dent. At the club I met *Capitaine* Maréchal, a fighter pilot in the *Armée de l' Air*, his charming wife and her delightful sister, and 'Fifi' Fickinger, chief test pilot for Amiot, who became a great friend. I lost all of my uniform buttons but won a French one from Rosanoff (that I still wear on my tunic) and another from Maréchal. I don't remember going home, but I woke up in my own bed in the morning having slept through an *'Alerte'* in spite of the fact that the siren was right outside my window.

Apart from these trips 'abroad', we also managed to amuse ourselves locally. The various French units stationed round about asked us to dinner from time to time, and we used to invite them back for

---

* Later General Rosanoff, killed in 1954 demonstrating a new French jet fighter to the British Air Minister.

drinks in the mess (which was all we could manage as a rule). The general commanding a *Chasseur* brigade had his headquarters at Sermaize, a nearby village, and we occasionally dined with them. Here I made a great friend in Count Adalbert de Segonzac.

I found the going somewhat sticky once, sandwiched between two colonels and facing the general. But after dinner the general and the senior officers usually withdrew and things would warm up considerably. Great singers these Frenchmen! Mostly they sang marches or ballads glorifying the manly arts of love and war.

When the Frenchmen came to see us we would enthusiastically ply them with beer or whisky, or both. Two officers of the *Chasseurs-Alpins*, Pérez and Dubois, came often. Pérez was a strong, good-looking young fellow, fit as a fiddle, with a head of teak. Dubois, on the other hand, though wiry and tough, had no head for English liquor. On his first visit – at lunchtime – he downed such quantities of the lethal beer-and-whisky mixture that he had to be carried out at six o'clock that evening to a waiting car. Pérez discreetly put him to bed when they got back and made his excuses to the general. I never saw Pérez remotely affected, even after eight hours of 'Cardinal Puff' when he became a triple cardinal – in whisky, brandy and cointreau, rounding it off triumphantly with several cocktails of all three mixed together!

A French bomber reconnaissance wing, the 33rd *Groupe*, was based a few miles south of us. The 1st *Escadrille* of this unit was based on St Dizier, commanded by *Commandant* Valin, and they had put up some very good shows on trips into Germany. The squadron was equipped with Potez 637s, and had quite a few brushes with the Messerschmitts even before Christmas 1939. One of them on such a trip had come down to 50 feet over the Frankfurt streets while being chased, thus preventing the German fighters from opening fire. This Squadron was singled out for special mention by the French High Command early in the war, and at the same time was decorated with two *Croix de Guerre*, plus a *Légion d'Honneur* for Valin.*

1 Squadron was invited to the special dinner to celebrate this occasion at St Dizier. All of us were feeling particularly cold, tired and fed-up on the evening in question, and none of us was over-keen to

---

*Valin was later appointed to the command of the Free French Air Force in London and promoted to General.

turn out in the rain, changed, and face a long cold drive in the van. Consequently there were no volunteers. As I spoke French Johnny asked me to go. I felt it would be a poor show for only one of us to turn up, so I nagged Johnny, Killy and Boy into coming with me.

We bolted off to our billets, spruced up and eventually arrived at the hotel where the French squadron had their mess. We were feeling pretty glum as we trailed into the big mess-room, with its lavishly set centre table, the bar hung with the *tricolore* and the inevitable squadron artist's very passable efforts. But after the formal presentation to Major Valin the champagne began to flow and we were introduced to a group of very attractive young ladies. Things were looking up.

After more champagne accompanied by jazz from the radio-gramophone the scene looked positively agreeable. We sat down to dinner actually feeling quite jolly. I was placed next to Guy d' Eclosière, who spoke English carefully and well. I spent my time during the three courses rehearsing a speech I intended to make, and Guy was invaluable in providing me with the form of address to use and so on. The dinner at last came to an end, and having fortified myself with a last desperate gulp of champagne, I rose to my feet.

There was silence. *'Mesdames, mon Président, Messieurs,'* I said in the loud and, I hoped, clear tones befitting the occasion, continuing in French: 'First we want to thank you for the great welcome you have given us. Second, we would like to congratulate you for the citations and decorations you have so bravely won, and we are very happy to be here to celebrate the occasion with you. On behalf of the First fighter squadron of the Royal Air Force, I raise my glass and wish "Good luck" to the First squadron of the 33rd *Groupe* of the *Armée de l'Air!'* Tremendous applause greeted these few words, and I sat down from my first public speech, satisfied if embarrassed, to the roar of some peculiar phrase the company was shouting at me. *'Pour vous, ça!'* said Guy, and I thanked him for his generous cooperation: it was really his speech.

Speeches were followed by songs, and inevitably an English song was called for. We exchanged fearful looks. The English, I thought belatedly, are singularly ill-versed in the social graces. Then, on a silly inspiration, I rose to my feet again. In serious tones, amid dead silence, I said: 'The English are a very musical race. And that is why we never sing. . .' I sat down quickly, thinking I had fumbled it. But a momentary hesitation was followed by a roar of laughter that continued for some minutes.

After dinner we danced, drank more champagne, and danced again. Eventually, Johnny having been stood on his head and having passed out in the bottom of the car with Boy, we took our boisterous leave in the car of Squadron Leader Pemberton from Wing headquarters. All I can remember about the journey back was that it seemed extremely rapid and that the following conversation took place:

'Not so fast, Paul,' said Pemberton.

'OK,' said I.

Three minutes later.

'Ease off a bit, old boy,' said Pemberton.

'OK,' said I.

Three minutes later.

'Hey, I'm not driving, you bloody fool, you are!' I said.

'Am I?' said Pemberton. 'Oh, so I am!'

We saw the Potez squadron quite often after that night, and I flew a Hurricane down for them to look over. The weather turned nasty and I couldn't stay long, but I beat them up in the rain before leaving.

Coming back from patrols we sometimes beat up Velaine, between Toul and Nancy, where the Lafayette Wing was stationed. Incidentally, we thought the Lafayette boys were a bunch of line-shooters: by the time their wing's score had reached twenty most of them had the *Croix de Guerre* and the unit was sent to Cannes on a month's leave! To 1 and 73, who each had equivalent scores and not a single decoration, this seemed a curious way of fighting a death struggle with the world's most formidable military power . . .*

One winter's day I went up alone on a high local patrol. On the way back I went over and had a look at St Dizier, all black-and-white in the snow. I came down fast out of a bleak sky, rolling, looping and stall-turning. When I got down to 5,000 feet I saw a Potez taking off, blowing a cloud of snow out behind it. I dived on it as it circled the airfield slowly and shot over it at about 400 mph. As I pulled up

---

* We did not know that it was established French practice to award the *Croix de Guerre* for a fighter pilot's first victory and a palm to it for each thereafter. In retrospect a working holiday at Cannes seems a jolly good way to freshen up before a battle!

to one side, I noticed that the Potez's undercarriage was still down and that it was flying very slowly, so I didn't bother it again and watched closely as it approached to land. It crossed the hedge too fast and I watched for the cloud of snow as it touched down, but it had floated three-quarters of the way across the airfield before I saw its wheels kick up a puff, then another puff as they touched again, followed by a series of puffs, then a steady stream, as the aircraft bounced and ran straight off the airfield at a good 70 mph. I laughed at the slapstick effect as it missed a small house by inches, knocked down a couple of trees and ended up swinging round and knocking its tail off on another tree. Luckily there was no fire, and I dived low to see if anyone got out. They did – smartly – and as I dived a second time they waved good-naturedly; I nearly hit the poplars along the road waving back. I later found my friend Pierre Scordel had been in the aircraft, and the cause of the accident was a cut engine and a bad one-engine landing. They were damned lucky to get away with it.

I first met Pierre at the St Dizier party, when I christened him and his delightful Hungarian wife Mary 'the love birds'. Before the war he had travelled extensively in Europe and North Africa in his own aeroplane, and had married Mary in Budapest on the eve of the war. Being a reserve officer in the *Armée de l'Air*, Pierre immediately headed for France by the quickest route – through Germany. By the time they reached the Rhine Germany had attacked Poland and destroyed all the bridges. Pierre appealed to the local *Luftwaffe* station. The *Luftwaffe* behaved in a most civilised manner and entertained Mary and Pierre (now in full *Armée de l'Air* uniform) in their mess. They entirely understood that an officer should wish to report for duty when war was imminent, and escorted the couple to the end of a blown-up bridge and shouted to the French sentries on the other side that they had a French officer who wished to cross. Not unnaturally the French soldiers received this news with some derision. But the enterprising Germans launched a boat and rowed Pierre and Mary across the Rhine under a white flag. The next day France declared war on Germany.

We only gave an organized dinner for the French once because some of us always had to be on the airfield before dawn next morning. On this one occasion we sent an invitation to all the French units who had entertained us, and a few representatives came from each. The dinner was not exactly a roaring success as very few of us spoke French, and the Bull was at the best of times rather tactless with our allies; he was quite frank about it: he just didn't like them. After dinner an *Armée de l'Air* captain, evidently feeling something must be done to cheer things up, performed conjuring and card tricks, choosing me as his subject. He was an exceptionally skilful and amusing fellow. Tall and heavily built, with black hair thinning on top, a humorous mouth and dark, prominent eyes with curiously heavy lids, I discovered later that he was the famous author and poet, Antoine de Saint-Exupéry.

We were now being entertained by concert parties once a week – although Air Headquarters at Reims had been diverted by them all through the winter! They were fairly pedestrian shows, so we reopened the cinema at Bar-le-Duc. But our most popular relaxation was to visit the Hotel de Metz at Bar-le-Duc and have a hot bath and a marvellous dinner. The Metz was an ordinary-looking French provincial hotel, but exceptionally well run by Madame Ensminger, her son Jean and his Breton wife, known affectionately to us as Madame Jean. Here the food and wine were excellent and the prices reasonable. Here we would always find a welcome and a refuge from the cold. Here we entertained what guests we had from time to time. Here we would celebrate our occasional victories. And here I would love to retreat for the evening with a chosen companion and, over a good dinner and a bottle of wine, discuss – well, anything – anything but the war.

Madame Jean was regarded as a member of the Squadron, and always referred to it as 'our Squadron'. Over a period of time she collected a set of RAF buttons, one from each of us, which she proudly wore on a little blue coat with the wings and crown from an officer's field service cap; she painstakingly gathered together an album of photographs of each one of us, and insisted that we sign them. How heart-broken she was when one of us was killed! And how jubilant at each of our victories! She became very depressed on hearing rumours that our departure was imminent, but cheered herself and us up with the promise that on our return – and return we must – the Hotel de Metz would put on a never-to-be-forgotten gala dinner to celebrate. She was as good as her word.

In January 1940 I was sent up to 'Wing' – 67 Wing Headquarters, commanded by Wing Commander Walter and located in a pleasant house in a village two miles from our own – Bussy-la-Côte. As its name suggests the village stood on a hillside, overlooking a valley through which ran our stream, railway and canal, and almost facing the far end of the airfield. My duties in the operations room were not arduous, and I shared them with Squadron Leader Pemberton, our chief operations officer, and a pilot from 73 Squadron. I was glad to be there, for the weather was bitterly cold and the countryside smothered with snow and ice. We were unable to fly, and I could live in a warm house with good food and a comfortable sitting room.

My ample time off-duty was consumed in reading, writing my diary, and playing a strange breed of soccer with the Padre, Henry (the army signals officer) and the troops. Sometimes I meandered along the valley, occasionally taking photographs. One day I came across an old deserted house and took some shots of beautiful abstract ice formations clinging round a waterfall in the grounds.

Sleuthing after spies was another diversion. One of our technical officers had spy mania and was convinced there was a jamming machine in the village interfering with the Squadron's R/T. There certainly was jamming when we were trying to intercept enemy aircraft, but it probably came from Germany. However, this keen chap was sure it was local and strongly suspected a certain house kept by a strange lady who had a pack of savage dogs in her garden. He crept about the village in the dead of night, climbing her wall and generally snooping about. He said the dogs were being deliberately starved to make them fierce, and was convinced she had something to hide. Accordingly he visited the dogs every night, fed them, and gradually tamed them. After a while they didn't even bark when his eager form dropped over the wall. But after all his painstaking investigations he found nothing.

Another rather rum local character was the blind professor. It seemed he had been a professor at the University of Nancy, but had been evacuated to Bussy for some obscure reason. He lived in a small room next to the garage that adjoined our house and busied himself typing in Braille all day and far into the night. The curious thing was that whenever a car passed he had no trouble in running outside, which meant negotiating two doorways and a flight of steps. He

Flying Officer Paul Richey, DFC and Bar. *Cecil Beaton.*

A Hawker Fury of 1 Squadron airborne over Tangmere in 1937; one man, 695 horsepower and two slow-firing Vickers machine guns. The Squadron was mounted on Furies from 1929 to 1939. *Charles Crusoe.*

World Champions

1 Squadron's 1937 formation aerobatic team practising near Tangmere and starting

. . . a stall turn

. . . a roll and

. . .a loop. *Charles Crusoe.*

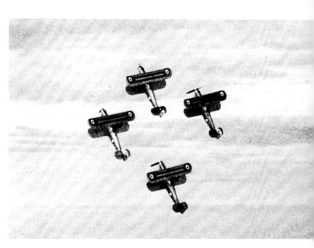

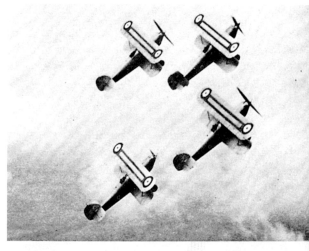

Preparing for war

After Munich: the Hurricanes of 1 Squadron's 'B' Flight on morning parade, Tangmere, spring 1939. One man, 1,030 horsepower and eight quick-firing Browning machine guns to each aircraft. Note the two-bladed fixed-pitch wooden propellers. *Author*.

'How gay they looked with their red, white and light-blue markings! But how pathetically out of date.' One of the Amiot 143 heavy bombers of the *Armée de l'Air* intercepted by 1 Squadron on its way to 'attack' London during the RAF's last air exercise before the war: five men, 1,800 horsepower, four machine guns and 1,300 kilograms of bombs. *Ét Ciné-Armées*.

Sitzkrieg

After three weeks of good Norman living at Le Havre we felt more than ready to take on the Germans where our fathers had left off in 1918. (Right to left) Boy Mould, Stratters Stratton and I celebrate orders to move to the BEF 'front' on the Belgian border. *Author*.

Air France, the French national airline, unlike its British counterpart, Imperial Airways, was mobilized with France's armed forces. Here a bunch of Air France aircrew come with their Wibault T.12s to lift our advance party from Norrent-Fontes to Vassincourt in the active war zone in eastern France. *Author*.

The Wibault T.12 ammunition lift in which *Capitaine* Casanova and I were shot up by British guns over Arras – the only action we saw with the Air Component of the BEF. *Author.*

Not so 'phoney' for some...

French fighters and reconnaissance aircraft went into action over Germany at the very beginning of the war when the French Army advanced in limited support of Poland. The Germans riposted defensively with armed reconnaissance. On 8 September 1939 – the day 1 Squadron landed at Le Havre – seven out of nine French bombers of this type, the Bloch 200, were shot down by Me 109s during a daylight reconnaissance of Trier in Germany. *Ét Ciné-Armées.*

A Dornier Do 17 only just makes it to a German airfield after being attacked by French fighters during a reconnaissance mission over France. *Bundesarchiv*.

The crew only just make it too! The Luftwaffe's medical section treated urgent burn cases immediately and on the spot. *Bundesarchiv*.

A Heinkel 111 doesn't make it and is shot down by French fighters near Metz. *Ét Ciné-Armées*.

Others are even less lucky. The Germans bury the crew of a Heinkel 111.

Lt. Jean Sueur
2/Aufkl Geschwader 551
allen als tapferer Gegner, 11.9.39 Trussem

Capitaine Jean Rossignol
2./Aufkl. Geschwader 551
chevalier de la Legion d honneur
gefallen als
tapferer Gegner
11.9.39
Trassem

Two officers of 'the gallant foe' shot down over Germany in their Mureaux 117 observation aircraft on 11 September 1939, while covering the French Army's attack in support of Poland. *Bundesarchiv.*

Flying Officer Paul Richey's Hurricane 'dear old G' ready for a gun test over the Maginot Line.

Posing in front of 'G' before take-off with his fitter and rigger. *Author*.

Paul Richey with his beloved 'G'. Without runways the Hurricanes were usually badly mud-spattered.

The RAF's first victory in France since 1918 – Boy Mould (left) with the machine gun and oxygen bottle salvaged from the Dornier he shot down on 30 October 1939; the Bull (centre), Soper (right foreground) and Hilly Brown (behind him) with the trophies from their victories of 23 November. *IWM.*

Below, left: 'The man who came to dinner', photograph given to 1 Squadron by *Unteroffizier* Arno Frankenberger when he dined in our officers' mess on 25 November 1939, after shooting down, and being shot down by, Pussy Palmer two days earlier. *Arno Frankenberger.*

Below, right: Frankenberger's message dated 25 November 1939 on the back of the photograph: Zum Ewigen Andenken aus einem unterlegenen (signed) Arno Frankenberger – Leider – A.F.,' 'With eternal thanks on the part of a vanquished (signed) Arno Frankenberger – What a pity – A.F.'

The coldest winter for a century virtually stopped all flying for a time, but we and the French did get off rarely, although not always successfully. From the air I saw this crash in the snow on St Dizier airfield. Capitaine Pierre Scordel of the 33rd Groupe's 1st Escadrille with crew beside his Potez 637 afterwards. *Pierre Scordel.*

German fighters had their own problems: Me 109s have to be wheeled out on a thawing and flooded German airfield. *IWM.*

Prelude to a journey to the Rhine: Pierre and Mary's wedding in Budapest in 1939. They were soon to part forever: when the Germans attacked and Pierre's squadron became heavily engaged, Mary fled to Bordeaux, where she died giving premature birth to their son. On the back of the photograph is written: 'Budapest – le 22 Avril, 1939 – affectueux souvenir de vos 'love's birds', et de St. Didier – 25 November, 1939 – Pierre Scordel.'

Flight Lieutenant Prosser Hanks lands his two-blader at Vassincourt after a routine patrol over the Maginot Line; his No 2 is in a three-blader on his right. *IWM*.

Not much was left of Sergeant Clowes's tail after a Morane had clipped it.

My prop after it had disintegrated at 20,000 feet. *Author*.

Sergeant Clowes, myself and Johnny Walker enjoy a little 'sight-seeing' outside our mess at the Mairie with a recently shot-down Dornier's rear-gun. *IWM.*

The Advanced Air Striking Force of the Royal Air Force comprised only three types of aircraft: the Hurricane (fighter), Battle and Blenheim (bombers).

A flight of 73 Squadron's Hurricanes joining up into close echelon starboard, April 1940. All six are newly equipped with de Havilland three-bladed constant-speed propellers. Note the absence of squadron identification letters (those worn are for aircraft identification) and the red-white-and-blue rudder flashes (corresponding with the *Armée de l'Air's* blue-white-red markings), both exclusive to 1 and 73 Squadron in France. *IWM.*

A Battle gunner's view of a section of 73 Squadron's Hurricanes 'attacking' in abnormally close-formation for the photographer. The normal fighter breakaway was a peel-off down to one side to avoid return fire. We believed our Hurricanes to be a match for anything the Germans could put up, especially in a dogfight, but were aware of their inferiority to the German fighters in speed, climb and ceiling. *IWM.*

A section of Battles in close line-abreast near Reims. 12 Squadron lost twenty-six complete aircrews in action in the battle – seventy-eight highly trained men – but they were never grounded. *IWM.*

A 'vic' of 139 Squadron's Bristol Blenheim IV twin-engined bomber/reconnaissance aircraft: three men, 1,990 horse-power, two machine guns and 450 kilograms of bombs to each aircraft. This squadron lost most of its crews and all but three aircraft in action in the first week of the battle and was withdrawn. *IWM.*

A French fighter pilot ready to board his Morane 406. Note back-type parachute giving full mobility, strong, heated overalls, hygienic, efficient oxygen mask and goggles, and neat crash helmet. Only his radio control box is awkwardly slung - but it worked better than ours. *Ét Ciné-Armées*.

The Morane M.S. 406 fighter: one man, 850 horsepower, two machine guns and a cannon. Smaller, lighter and with less power than our Hurricane, the Morane nevertheless climbed much better, had a higher ceiling and its cannon packed more punch. The lightness, wide undercarriage and three-bladed constant-speed propeller made it eminently suitable for small grass airfields. *Ét Ciné-Armées*.

An *Armée de l'Air* Fighter Squadron Morane 406 comes to Vassincourt to show us its paces. Having had my first 'combat' with a Morane flown by a former French aerobatic squadron pilot I was not surprised by its manoeuvrability, but it impressed the rest of 1 Squadron. Watching the instruments with his mechanic, the pilot runs up his engine. *Author.*

A tight vertical turn all the way round the inside of the airfield perimeter at 30 feet . . . *Author.*

. . . and a controlled flick-roll at 100 feet. Cobber Kain was the only one of us who habitually performed this manoeuvre at that height – to his cost. *Author.*

The American-built Curtiss P-36 single-engined fighter was considerably more powerful than the Morane and almost as manoeuvrable, but was larger and heavier: one man, 1,200 horsepower and either four or six machine guns. Here *Commandant* Challe, French fighter liaison officer, boards his six-gun job at Vassincourt. *Author.*

Three Potez 63.11 bomber/reconnaissance aircraft fly into battle. With identical power plants to the Potez 637, this greatly improved type carried three crew, 200 kg of bombs and 12 machine guns.

The Mureaux 117 observation aircraft: two men, 860 horsepower and two machine guns. Hardly France's most advanced aeroplane, the Mureaux was nevertheless flown in large numbers with great courage in the face of strong German fighter and flak opposition for the sake of the French Army. I was personally grateful for a lift in one during the battle. *Ét Ciné-Armées.*

would then look up and down the road to see what it was. Then one day the telephones were somehow wrongly routed, and operational messages from AHQ at Reims to our ops room came through to the telephone in the garage – which the professor was extremely nimble in answering. I was quite certain the man was a spy, but no one seemed to bother about him. The French police had him on their list of suspects and probably were watching him in their own fashion.

There were certainly some fishy goings-on round Wing and our village – we even had a character, ostensibly a tourist, wandering about Neuville openly photographing our transport. The troops thought nothing of it, and by the time he was reported to an officer he had taken off. Another time, poor old Pemberton appeared in the mess looking deathly pale and announced that someone had fired a shot at him as he came up the steps. We never found out who it was.

On another occasion I escorted a new armament officer from Wing to the Squadron at Neuville. We were driven down a short-cut back road, and I had intended to leave the armament officer and hurry back to supper. But after a few drinks in the mess with the boys I decided to stay and sent my driver back. On his return trip someone took a pot shot at the car from a thicket near the road. The bullet smashed the windscreen right in front of where I would have been sitting and lodged in the door. The alarmed driver lay doggo, pistol in hand, but nothing happened so he drove on fast. The French police followed it up but found nothing.

The short-cut was now forbidden after dark, but I took it several times on foot to see what went on. One night I saw a bonfire blazing away in the wood and crept up to have a closer look. It was in a clearing, and a man was throwing branches on it. I approached him and asked what he was doing. He said he was an Italian wood cutter and that he lived in the forest. He invited me along to his house, and as I was armed I went. I wasn't too happy about the long axe the man shouldered. His house, his wife, and no less than nine children looked beguilingly innocent, but I reported him next day. It was a remote possibility that he had been signalling to German aircraft.

All our fears and suspicions seem quite absurd at a distance, even childish, but there undoubtedly were bizarre events taking place in France at this time. The French security service uncovered a telephone line direct to Germany under a stationmaster's office at

Châlons-sur-Marne, and we were not surprised to hear that four RAF officers and a couple of British dispatch riders were found at different times with their throats cut and uniforms stolen. I always carried a gun at night now, and slept with it beside me.

Yes, Bussy was an intriguing little village, with its air of mystery, of evil almost. But I prefer to remember it as I sometimes glimpsed it from the valley, with the evening sun glinting on its snow-covered roofs and gilding the square tower of its deserted little church.

Later, when the snows had melted, the countryside showed promise of blossoming into the wealth of fruit and flowers which provided the livelihood for the local people. '*Oui, le pays est très bon pour les fruits – et les fleurs et les poissons et tout et tout . . .*' Madame Chevailler, in whose farmhouse I was billeted, chattered. Monsieur Chevailler would arrive home from his work on the railway in the evening, pad along to my room and invite me to have a drink with him in the kitchen while he ate his supper.

'*Venez, Monsieur Richey*', he would say, '*venez boire un verre.*' He would fill my glass with red *vin ordinaire* and we would talk of the war. He would then become very earnest. '*Ah oui,*' he would grunt, shaking his head, '*ah oui - la guerre*'. Having finished his supper he would say '*Marie, la bouteille!*' As in a ritual Madame Chevailler would delve into the big kitchen chest and produce the Mirabelle. '*Vous prendrez une petite goutte Monsieur?*' he would ask as he poured me a glass. I could never refuse, and Madame would busy herself grinding and making coffee. Sometimes I would grind the coffee, then Madame would sit down with us as her husband became confidential.

'*Ah oui,*' he would say again, nodding sagely, continuing in French, 'and I can tell you that it will be very long.' He would then roll a cigarette slowly and deliberately.

'Oh, not as long as all that,' I would say with a shrug, 'three years – perhaps four.' He would look at me for a long moment as he puffed his cigarette. Then he would lean forward and tap my knee to punctuate what he was saying. 'I am not one of those who says things – and I know plenty. I am very discreet, you understand, and I don't tell everything I know. But you are a soldier and I can tell you that it will be very long and very hard. Ah yes!'

Although we were worlds apart in education and background, a great affection sprang up between my hosts and myself. Often the old boy would drag me out to the little *café* at the corner, or to the baker's down the road, where he took great delight in instructing me in novel and sometimes very unpleasant mixtures of alcohol. He was a short, rotund man, thickset and strong, with a round weather-beaten face, jet-black eyes and a walrus moustache. He was simple, sincere, with a wonderful sense of humour. His wife was a big untidy woman, loud and Rabelaisian. She would tell me jokes roaring with laughter and heartily slapping her thigh. But I sometimes caught her offguard, weeping quietly, thinking about her two sons at the front; then she would say simply *'Oui, j' ai le cafard aujourd'hui . . .'*

Both Monsieur and Madame Chevailler were of the solid old peasant stock that is the backbone of France: honest, hardworking, simple, kind-hearted and courageous; content with the life they had built up in their farmhouse, self-supporting (if with little to spare), living and dying in their little world – the village – and ready to defend it to the last.

But I cannot complete this sketch of our *ménage* without mention of Flandin, the big English setter 'worth 700 francs', who fiercely attacked all visitors and bit any stranger who touched him. Much to the Chevaillers' surprise Flandin and I became great friends. He would often trot along to see me in my room, and whenever I entered the house he would stand up on his hind legs, rest his paws on my chest and lick my face – a compliment he had hitherto only paid to his master.

When we left Neuville I wrote my former host a letter of thanks for his hospitality, enclosing a hundred-franc note to pay for my firewood, and requesting him to buy a bottle of good wine with the change and perhaps drink my health in it. He answered in French as follows, in violet ink and thin flowery handwriting:

I thank you very sincerely for your generosity, of which you are unable to partake; all the same, I would have so much liked to have seen you again, inasmuch as we get on very well together. As you say, 'C'est la guerre'.

You are an officer of merit, I myself am at my job as you know, with my two sons fighting against a monster that we must destroy at any cost, and I think that we shall succeed.

I enclose a letter to you from my son, who is deeply touched . . .

I and my wife wish you happiness and prosperity for the days to come.

I hope to see you again one of these days if you can manage it.

A staunch and true comrade gives you a friendly handshake for himself and for his family. *

* The Chevailler family were lucky to escape the holocaust. When I returned to Neuville after the war it was mainly populated with widows from two neighbouring villages: in 1944 the Germans had burnt them to the ground and shot all the men because the nearby forest of Trois-Fontaines was a British-run resistance centre. Neuville had been next on the German list but was saved by the American army.

V

TWITCHING NOSES

When I returned to the squadron in February the weather was still bad and the cold intense. With snow and ice everywhere it was impossible to keep warm indoors or out – even the ink in my bedroom froze. In the mess we kept a jumbo-size kettle simmering on the stove to make endless hot grogs. The winter throughout Europe was exceptionally cold, and patrolling at 25,000 feet with no heating, or sitting in a tent on the airfield from dawn to dusk, was not very amusing.

But in March it improved. Not having done much reconnaissance during the miserable weather, the Germans now made up for lost time and there was promise of action. Because of their position, 73 had more opportunity for this than we did, as the regular German route seemed to be across the Moselle at the corner of Luxembourg. The 73 boys often saw the Huns pass over their airfield, and brought one down now and then – though not often enough, we thought. But in March 1940 they had met the German Messerschmitt Me 109 fighters, which made us green with envy.

Cobber Kain, a New Zealander, was 73's most split-arse pilot. He often led a section forty miles or more into Germany, regardless of the fact that it was against orders to cross the frontier. But on one occasion disaster struck the section relieving him on patrol. The Huns had seen Cobber and Co. floating about, and when a none-too-experienced pilot officer relieved him with two inexperienced sergeants just out from England, the 109s were waiting. The two new boys were shot down in flames and killed, and the pilot officer was bloody lucky to get away. Cobber himself had some miraculous escapes, being twice shot down in flames in his first five combats.

Fanny Orton was one of 73's more experienced pilots and a very fine one. In March he attacked a formation of twenty-seven 109s single-handed, having to climb to reach them and shooting down two before escaping in cloud. He got the Distinguished Flying Cross for that action.

1 Squadron was getting very impatient for action by this time, and cursed its lousy luck at not having seen any German fighters. But it still remained the Squadron's policy to be cautious and bide its time. We seldom crossed the German frontier, and when we did we went over as high as possible and did a sweep round and back again to draw the enemy fighters out. If we saw a Hun, we'd cross the lines and attack if he was within reasonable distance, and we'd always chase across if there was a chance of catching one. But the Bull gave strict orders that there was to be no fooling about, no 'dare-devil ace' stuff. To eliminate temptation he excluded the brigade of press correspondents in France from contact with the Squadron. This was a training period, and very useful experience; our turn would come with the German push, said the Bull, and when it did we would be more than ready as a cohesive and disciplined team.

On 2 March we had our fifth victory. Hilly, Soper and Mitchell, a new pilot, were on patrol near Nancy when they sighted a Dornier 17. For no discernible reason, at this moment Hilly's wooden prop broke into pieces, and he force-landed on Nancy aerodrome with his wheels up. Soper and Mitchell attacked the Dornier alternately from astern. Soper was still at it when he heard Mitchell call: 'I'm hit in the engine and must go down!', so he left the Dornier, which was on fire and later crashed, and returned to find a field for Mitchell, who couldn't see through his smoke. Soper chose a field, watched Mitch approach, then lost sight of him completely. He flew back to Vassincourt and landed. We learned later that Mitch had spun in on the edge of the field and was killed. This was our first casualty of the war. Mitchell was a New Zealander, a big cheerful boy, and a Catholic. He lent me his pen the night before his death and I wrote this account with it.

The following day came our sixth victory, and Hilly and Soper were again involved. They sighted a Heinkel at 24,000 feet between Nancy and Metz. Hilly climbed level with and some distance from it, but Soper tried to attack from underneath and spun. Hilly managed to climb above it and closed in from astern in a dive, Soper climbed back again, and between them they set fire to both the Heinkel's engines and saw it crash-land between the French and German lines. Two men crawled out of the crippled aircraft and bolted for the German side, which they appeared to reach. When Hilly came to this part of the story I said 'I hope they made it.' Hilly's moustache fairly bristled with indignation. '*I* hope *not!*' he said emphatically. Perhaps I would have felt the same if I had been in the fight!

With better weather and the increase in enemy reconnaissance my own nose was twitching for a fight, as I had not yet had one. One morning I was leading a section comprising Stratters and Sergeant Clowes over Metz. The day was beautifully clear and the whole country lay spread before us, from Luxembourg round past the Hunsrück, the Rhine, the Vosges and the Black Forest to the blue horizon, where the snowy peaks of the Swiss Alps gleamed.

Suddenly I spotted some dots to the north, and warning the others I headed for them, climbing hard. Clowes got engine trouble and turned back. Stratters was still there and on we went. As we got nearer I saw more and more dots, and I swallowed hard. One – two – three – good Lord, a whole squadron – two squadrons! Well, we've got the sun – let's climb up and surprise them. As we approached still nearer I counted about forty dots. I looked round for Stratters. Yes, there he was, good man. I looked for the Huns again. Funny, most of them had disappeared . . . no – there were a whole lot more! But the others were now fading away. 'Well, you are an oaf,' I grinned to myself, 'it's ack-ack!' Still, they must be shooting at something. But we never found it. The ack-ack faded, and we swung south and dived from our 27,000-foot ceiling down to where it was warmer and easier to fly.

Then I got another shock – a large formation of bombers going north-east from Nancy at 15,000 feet, about twenty of them, with a dozen covering fighters. We got up into the sun behind them and zig-zagged along watching and getting into position to attack the fighters at speed and regain our height. But they were Frenchmen, flying in no particular formation, most of the escort straggling all over the sky. They were Mureaux reconnaissance aircraft and Morane fighters going into Germany. I wondered how many would come back. We loitered about hoping some 109s would come back with them, but although we heard later that there was a big battle, we saw nothing of it.

Before turning for home I saw condensation trails high over the Vosges. Petrol was low, so I sent Stratton home and climbed towards the distant white snakes in the sky. I soon decided the aircraft making them was a fighter, as it was going round in circles, diving and climbing as only a fighter would, and moving fast. As I drew nearer, I saw two aircraft, then a third. I climbed at full throttle into the sun to attack the leader. As I dived towards him he saw me, but I too saw that all three were French Curtisses, and we swung past each other in steeply banked turns, rocking our wings urgently in recognition.

I returned home cold and disappointed, but somehow more confident for not having funked it in the face of superior numbers of what I took to be the enemy, and for having stalked and surprised them in a clear sky from an inferior position. This sort of exercise made a considerable difference to us later on. The experience was cheap, realistic, exciting and invaluable. By the time things really started popping we were wily and comparatively seasoned fighters.

I took off alone one afternoon to test my guns at 25,000 feet, and headed towards the lines to fire them into Germany. On the way I climbed through a couple of cloud layers, but it was clear over Nancy and I could see the Moselle curving and gleaming away north towards Metz. I continued to climb, keeping a sharp look-out, but it was hard to remember there was a war on. I crossed the lines at 27,000 feet. There was a blanket of cloud below me between the frontier and Nancy at 10,000 feet, and another starting some distance the other side of the frontier and stretching away, flat and soft and peaceful, into the heart of Germany. The country below for some distance on either side of the frontier showed no signs of life; no smoke from the chimneys, no traffic on the roads, no barges on the canals. Towns and hills, winding rivers and dark-green rolling forests were below me; flat, white cloud layers, blue sky and brilliant sun above them; and far away to the south-east – some three hundred miles – I could again see the white peaks of the Alps.

All this filled me with the unique sensation of remoteness that only the pilot knows. It often requires a strong physical effort to wrench oneself out of this high-altitude dreaming, and the mind tends to wander in a curious way. Doctors say it is lack of oxygen, but I believe there are other causes. At any rate, I was hunting and could not afford to let my mind wander; so I concentrated my thoughts once more on the watchers on the ground, on the anti-aircraft guns, and on the stalking 109s. I turned my Hurricane constantly from one side to the other, sometimes doing a complete circle, and twisted my head round continuously, searching every corner of the sky, paying special attention to my tail and to that bright but treacherous sun. Now and again I fired my guns and was comforted to feel the shudder of the aircraft and to see the converging streams of incendiaries spurt out ahead.

After floating round Saarbrücken and about forty miles inside Germany for half an hour I turned for home. The clouds were thicker below and I decided to come down over Verdun, as I thought. I dived through several layers of thick cloud and found myself above a final layer at 1,000 feet. I went through a hole gently to find it very dark underneath and visibility bad. I then saw a fair-sized town and flew over it without recognizing it. Shortly afterwards I saw another town, with an aerodrome. On the edge was a hospital prominently marked with the red cross, and in the centre of the field was a circle with ESCH lettered in white in the middle. I couldn't locate Esch on the map and didn't like the sound it made, so I flew away. Petrol was low, so I flew south for another few minutes and looked for another airfield. I found a town that had one, but it looked small, and I decided to try to get home. I thought the town must be Ste Mene-hould, but after flying down a valley past factories and railway lines I made up my mind to accept the fact that I was lost and returned to the last airfield. I was by now so short of petrol that I made a forced-landing approach to be on the safe side. The airfield was so boggy I nearly turned over. I taxied in to find I was at Thionville.

Esch, I discovered, was in Luxembourg, and the town I flew over was the capital, so I nearly emulated Dicky Martin of 73 Squadron, the 'Prisoner of Luxembourg'. Incidentally, Dicky's escape was very amusing. After his imprisonment he was exercised daily in an open space by an officer. He induced the officer to buy him a map of Luxembourg on the pretext of being interested in the history and topography of the country. Christmas Day dawned foggy and Dicky laid his plan. He displayed such vigour at his exercising, doubling back and forth enthusiastically, that his guard got tired out and stopped. Dicky asked his permission to trot on, and continued alone, to and fro, supervised by the fed-up officer. He went on and on, back and forth, each time moving a little farther away before turning. At length he just walked straight off, was swallowed up in the fog, ran like the devil and managed to reach France after several days on the loose. He was nearly shot as a spy but eventually made it back to his squadron.

At last, on 29 March, 1 Squadron met the German fighters, I had my first fight, and we scored our seventh victory. Seven always was my lucky number and this time it was again.

I was on patrol near Metz at nine in the morning with Pussy leading and Pete Mathews No 3 behind me. At 20,000 feet I sighted flak north-east at 15,000 feet, and flew towards it as Pussy couldn't see it. Pussy then spotted the aircraft that was drawing the flak. I never saw it and Pussy lost it shortly afterwards. We were searching vainly, by now at 25,000 feet, when I saw two 109s left above us flying in the opposite direction. I reported them and we climbed to attack, but suddenly Pete called 'Look out behind!' Three other 109s were attacking from the rear. Pete behind me was fired at and blacked out pulling out of the way, coming to at 10,000 feet. Pussy ahead of me dived steeply left, spiralled and then spun. Thinking Pussy had mistaken me for a Hun I called 'It's only me!', but I was alone by then and continued to climb in a left-hand turn, watching my tail. I saw an aircraft climbing up behind me, but wasn't sure whether he was friend or foe so waited to see whether he opened fire. He did, at longish range, and I twisted down underneath his nose. As I flattened out violently, either he or one of the 109s I had seen above dived on my port side and whipped past just above my cockpit. He was so close that I heard his engine and felt the air-wave, and I realized that he must have lost sight of me in the manoeuvre. He pulled up in front of me, stall-turned left and dived steeply in a long, graceful swoop with me on his tail. He was much faster and I couldn't get within range, so I held my fire. He went down about 10,000 feet, pulled up violently at an angle of fifty degrees or so, then throttled back at the top of a long straight climb, and I started gaining on him.

Waiting until he was in range and sitting pretty, I let him have it. My gun button was sticking and I wasted ammunition, but he started to stream smoke. The pilot must have been hit, for he took no evasive action, merely falling slowly in a vertical spiral. I was very excited and dived on top of him using my remaining ammunition. I then pulled out and saw another 109 about 2,000 feet above me. He headed for me, but knowing his speed to be superior I didn't dive away but turned on him, partly to stop him getting on my tail, and partly to bluff him. Either he had finished his hardware (which was unlikely, for the Germans carried 1,000 rounds for each gun to our 300) or he'd witnessed his chum's fate and wasn't feeling so brave. Anyway, he beat it – and so did I, at ground level until I reached Nancy. I calculated my 109 must have fallen near Merzig in Germany, and it therefore could not be confirmed from the ground. Bad luck.

A little later the same day, Johnny eclipsed my victory over the Squadron's first enemy fighter by getting the first Messerschmitt 110 to fall to Allied fighters. With Stratton and Clowes he sighted nine of them, the first to appear over France, north of Metz. The Hurricanes climbed to attack. Johnny stuck behind one through some violent manoeuvres and first-class flying – vertical stall-turns and so on. He followed it through cloud, saw it catch fire, and ran out of ammunition. It was later found in pieces, the pilot having parachuted out. Sergeant Clowes had a bang at two others, but was uncertain of the results. Stratton attacked another.

Air Marshal 'Ugly' Barratt, who commanded the British Air Forces in France, had a few days previously issued an invitation to dine with him in Paris to the first pilot to shoot down a Messerschmitt 110 on the Western Front. The Air Marshal's personal aircraft, a Percival Q-6, collected Johnny, Stratton and Clowes the day after their successful engagement with the 110s. The Air Marshal turned on a slap-up dinner at Maxim's for them – quite rightly, I thought.

On the evening of these two fights, as was the custom, the victors ceremoniously drank from the special bottle of rum reserved for these occasions, with the toast 'To past members of 1 Squadron!', and filled in and signed the Victory Card. A party was not long in materializing, and we 'passed out' via the sergeants' mess, which was particularly cosy and done up like an English country pub, with a bar, beer-barrel seats and a wide open hearth. I went across to the village church opposite the mess to say a prayer for the German pilot I had killed, before I got too boozy. The door was locked, so I knelt on the steps and prayed for him and his family, and for Germany.*

Prosser, Leslie and Boy ran into nine more 110s near Metz on the last day of March. They climbed to attack but the 110s dived on them, one opening fire head-on at Prosser, who replied. Prosser got a shell in the oil tank in his port wing, but continued the scrap, then force-landed at 73's airfield at Rouvres. After the engagement each of our pilots claimed a 110.

On April Fools' Day Leslie, Lewis (a new Canadian pilot), Laurie (from 87 Squadron), Pussy and Killy went on patrol near Nancy. I was off late through starting trouble and lost them.

They sighted a Dornier and gave chase, but were attacked by five 109s. Pussy got a shell in his front petrol tank before he knew what was happening. He inverted his machine and baled out, his aircraft crashing in flames. He landed by parachute just three hundred yards inside the French lines and had a wild party with the local infantry regiment, the famous *Diables Rouges*. The other boys had a short, sharp clash, Killy getting a 109 (confirmed from the ground, but falling in Germany) and Leslie claiming another.

Meanwhile I was messing about at 25,000 feet north of Metz, where I thought the boys would be. All I saw were half a dozen Moranes and a heap of cloud. I dived through broken cloud, thinking I was near Thionville. At 9,000 feet I got peppered by quick-firers and took violent evasive action. I realized I was actually over Trier, thirty miles inside Germany, so I flew up the Moselle at no mean speed. I landed at Metz for petrol, but broke my tail-wheel taxiing in and was stuck there for two days.

I landed simultaneously with the Moranes I had seen. They had been in a fight and were highly excited, the victors being naturally especially jubilant. Their CO kindly sent a pilot to Vassincourt for my new tail-wheel and the excellent French mechanics had it on by nightfall. But the weather went sour so I stayed where I was.

* My prayer had already been answered: German records show my adversary was Leutnant Volk of the crack III/Jagdgeschwader 53, commanded and led by the famous ace Captain (later Colonel) Werner Mölders. I did not kill him: he crash-landed wounded near Saarburg.

I wandered in the gardens of Metz, admiring their special style of landscaping, and the women, who are renowned for their beauty. I toured round the cathedral and inside met a French army lieutenant, a tall, handsome man with deep-set grey eyes and a lean, hard face that had a curiously contradictory gentleness in it. *'Pardon, monsieur, sauriez-vous où on pourrait trouver un prêtre?'* I asked. 'No, I'm afraid I'm looking for a priest myself,' he replied in perfect English. So together we softly crept along the gloomy aisles beneath the soaring arches until we found a priest and made our confessions.

We met again later that evening at the *Réunion* (Officers' Club), where a formal dinner was being held in farewell to the general commanding the district. I borrowed a shirt and shoes to exchange for my roll-neck jersey and flying boots, but my old uniform looked pretty beaten-up. No one seemed to mind. Several British Army officers were present, and a British colonel made a fine speech in French. One magnificent old French warrior made a deep impression on me. He was of medium height, spare, with an arm missing and a wooden leg. He had flowing white hair, fine features, and keen and humorous blue eyes, and his vivacious manner was inspiring by its air of unquenchable courage. My friend from the cathedral sat beside me. His name was du Luart, and we found we had many mutual friends.

Dinner was followed by songs, and as the rifles and sabres on the walls of the great hall rattled to the roar of *'Saint-Cyr, Garde à Vous'*, *'La Madelon'*, *'Les Artilleurs de Metz'*, the *'Marche Lorraine'* and other stirring French war songs, we were transported back to the days when Metz was a gay garrison town whose cobbled streets rang to the clatter of cavalry and horse artillery, its cafés and restaurants crowded with brilliant uniforms. *'Roll out the Barrel'*, the British offering, proved a great favourite with the French. It's a good marching song, but lacks the *élan* of the French marches, and it dispelled our dreams of an army of long ago, jerking us back to the tanks and drab uniforms of modern warfare.

I left Metz in doubtful weather, and on reaching the Verdun valley found clouds on the hills and heavy rain. I tried flying along several valleys unsuccessfully, so flew up the Verdun valley with the intention of landing at 73's airfield at Rouvres. On reaching Verdun I realized I was trapped in the valley. I could have climbed into the clouds, hopped over the hills in them and come down on the other side, but I've known a lot of pilots make a mess of themselves that way. Luckily there was a small unused airfield at Verdun, so I landed there. I spent the night with 73 Squadron, and in the morning only got off that apology for an airfield with the aid of forty French troops, a half-gale and the boost-override plug pulled, missing the conveyor cables on the edge of the field by inches. Ten minutes later I landed at Vassincourt.

In the first week of April Pussy, Killy and I did our usual morning patrol round Metz and Nancy, and eastwards from there, but were disappointed as usual. On the way back we dog-fought among ourselves, then mildly beat-up Velaine, a French fighter base. I followed Pussy down close behind from 15,000 feet. We were knocking up a hell of a speed at the bottom of the dive, and Pussy was trailing black smoke from a wide-open throttle, so I broke the close formation and followed up behind him in a couple of climbing rolls. We left the forest of Toul behind us and slid lazily back in the sunshine to Bar-le-Duc to land at Vassincourt, taxi over to the tankers and refuel.

I jumped down to chat with Killy. We glanced at the sunny sky now and then from habit. There were a lot of condensation trails about, but mostly in the distance: visibility was perfect. Suddenly we heard the familiar sound of German engines and both looked up.

'There she is – a Hun all right!' I said, and pointed to the small but clearly visible outline of a Ju 88, its duck-egg blue underside glinting against the deeper blue of the sky. 'Twenty thousand, I'd say – slap over the airfield! *He'll* get some pretty pictures . . .' But Killy was already sprinting to his Hurricane, which was refuelled and running. He took off like a rocket, while I raced over to my machine, which wasn't quite ready. I suspended the refuelling, started up, and watched the Hun and Killy as I strapped in. I saw the German aircraft turn south, but for some reason Killy turned south-east. I took off hurriedly and climbed south-west, thinking I might cut the Hun off if he resumed his journey west. But I lost him taking off, and though I climbed to 20,000 feet I couldn't pick him up again.

My oxygen supply showed zero from take-off – there had been no time to renew it – but there was a little left and I used it sparingly and not until I reached 18,000. (Normally it was turned on at 15,000 at the highest.) I circled wide over Vitry-le-François and Châlons-sur-Marne, climbing and searching all the time. Not a sign: only a pattern of white trails to the north-east. I headed towards them, but the aircraft making them was too fast and too high. (The Bull later told me that it was him, testing his new Rotol-prop Hurricane.)

At 27,000 feet I was panting for oxygen, so I turned north of Ste Menehould towards Vassincourt. Now I was feeling definitely faint: my head buzzed, my brain and actions were sluggish and a dark veil pressed over my eyes. I remember saying urgently to myself: 'Come on, get down or you'll pass out!', and I dived at fifty degrees, forgetting to throttle back I was so dopey. At 20,000 feet I was smartly snapped out of my comatose state by a solid BANG that jarred the Hurricane. I throttled back immediately, thinking 'Christ! My bloody tail's coming off!' and eased out of the dive infinitely gently, screwing round anxiously to look at the tips of the tail plane, then at the cowlings on the guns and engine. Everything seemed OK, but I was losing speed unduly slowly. The prop perhaps . . . I opened the throttle a fraction. Yes, that's it – my prop's bust: the engine turned over roughly, then I felt a minor jolt as a last piece flew off the prop, and she ran perfectly smoothly. I throttled right back again, then cautiously opened the throttle, watching my rev counter. It whirled right round the clock to about 3,000, so I hastily snatched back the throttle and switched off. The entire prop had disintegrated. All this feverish activity took just a few seconds.

So there I was – no prop and twenty miles from the airfield; but from my 20,000 feet I could just make it out. I settled into a steady glide and arrived over it at 9,000 feet. I must say I felt pretty windy on the way down, with visions of finishing mangled in the far hedge or of spinning in. But on my last half-circuit, when I knew my position was just right and I could turn in anywhere I liked if necessary and make it, I began to enjoy the sensation of gliding silently through the air, with no prop turning over in front and obscuring the view, and no noisy engine vibrating the aircraft. Even so, when I climbed out at the end of my wheels-down landing run I found to my surprise that my hands were trembling.

I walked towards the pilots' hut and met Johnny, Prosser and Boy running across to me. I laughed when we met, and the noise sounded strange.

'Bloody prop's come off!' I said.

They laughed too, and Johnny punched me hard on the shoulder. 'What the hell did you do with it?' he asked.

'Nothing in particular – it just came off.'

Johnny was highly amused as I told them what had happened.

'We couldn't figure out what the blazes you were doing,' he said. 'We saw this Hurricane going round and round the airfield very slowly, then couldn't hear any engine noise when it got lower, so we thought some clown was trying to be clever and had switched his engine off. Anyway, bloody good show, Paul!'

'Yes, damn good show, Paul!' said Boy, with a grin. And Prosser made me feel really good by adding 'And a bloody good landing too!'

Meanwhile there was no sign of Killy, and as the morning wore on we rather forgot him. The telephone rang and Johnny took a section off on patrol. The rest of us lay about in the sun, playing the gramophone and reading. 'Moses' Demozay, our Breton interpreter, had contributed a pile of racy French magazines to the mess, which helped pass the time. I produced my clarinet and proceeded to make the morning hideous until, under dire threat of mutilation of my person, I retreated to a grassy bank behind the trees.

Our peace was broken by a sudden rush and roar. A Hurricane dived low over us and rocked its wings in the victory sign. We all jumped up to see Johnny's 'D' on its side. He landed and taxied over. We ran across to meet him as he waved and stuck his thumb up. I jumped up on his wing and noticed his normally calm brown eyes were exceptionally bright above his oxygen mask.

'What was it?' I shouted through the slipstream.

'A 109!' came the muffled answer. This was our seventh fighter victory.

At lunch we had news of Killy. He was near Paris and as stoned as an owl. That evening he was delivered back into the bosom of the Squadron and blurrily told his tale. He had kept the Hun – our first Ju 88 – in sight after taking off, lost him, but picked him up again. The Hun kept turning, and as Killy got nearer started climbing. Killy had his boost-override pulled all the time, and eventually was able to get quite near the Hun at 27,000 feet, still going west. At last he was close enough to open fire at long range, and the Ju 88 got the wind up and dived. They went down to ground level, Killy blazing away and getting in some close bursts low down. Suddenly Killy's engine was hit and 'blew up'. He crash-landed in great haste with his wheels up, travelling fast and on fire.

Killy leapt from his Hurricane, still in one piece, and was rescued by the French, who took him in charge and generously plied him with liquor. He was bloody annoyed at losing the Hun, but enjoyed a relaxing day with the French. Later on in the evening we learned that Killy had nailed his Ju 88 after all: it had crash-landed near Mâcon, miles south of where he had left it. The crew could not explain why they had flown the course they did when attacked, had no idea where they were, and had completely lost their bearings and their heads in the fight – which is not at all difficult to do. They had a list of fifteen towns to be photographed on their reconnaissance mission and had been to most of them when they unhappily met Killy.

A few days later an air marshal from the Air Ministry paid us a visit. He had come, he told us, to find out why we had shot down every aircraft we had attacked while the Fighter Command squadrons in England were, in the main, only succeeding in 'driving the German aircraft off in an easterly direction', as the communiqués delicately phrased it.

Since we were no longer under the jurisdiction of Fighter Command we had no hesitation in telling the air marshal the reason.

All single-seat eight-gun squadrons in Fighter Command – both Hurricanes and Spitfires – had very poor practice shooting results before the outbreak of war. We all used the 'Dowding Spread' at that time – a method of gun-harmonization laid down in accordance with the conviction of our Commander-in-Chief, Air Marshal Sir Hugh Dowding, that his fighters would never see, let alone engage, enemy fighters.

In theory the Dowding Spread, which was worked out for shooting at enemy bombers from astern, seemed a good idea. Used against a big target, theoretically it produced a wide enough bullet pattern to compensate for aiming error and left sufficient lethal density to destroy such a target. Furthermore, the range laid down – 400 yards – was outside effective enemy defensive fire.

Now we were not armament experts, but we knew about flying

and air firing, and we didn't like the Dowding Spread. We reckoned that, even if the experts were right and that at 400 yards' range the bullet velocity was still high enough to prevent tumble, maintain accuracy and penetrate armour (which seemed unlikely), the spread produced by aiming, shooting and random errors combined would be more than enough to drop lethal density below the minimum required for a kill, especially against a small target like a fighter – which *we* were not at *all* convinced we would never meet. As for defensive fire from an enemy bomber, we felt his one or two guns hardly stood a chance against the Hurricane's eight. Curiously, the only thing we were wrong about turned out to be this last point.

Fighter Command had dismissed our theories, so during our month's shooting practice in the spring of 1939 we secretly harmonized all our guns on a spot at 250 yards' range. Our shooting results on towed air targets showed we were right – we shot them clean away time and time again. Action in France had now proved the point: we had shot down every enemy aircraft we'd attacked.

To the air marshal, and later to the Air Staff, the case was conclusive. All single-seat fighter squadrons were instructed to adopt our method. It was not a moment too soon . . .

Not so long afterwards we made another contribution that was to benefit all our fighter squadrons. While still with Fighter Command, in order to facilitate recognition by our observers on the ground the undersides of our wings were painted black on one side, white on the other. We considered this to be idiotic, since the German aircraft were duck-egg blue underneath and very difficult to spot from below, whereas we stood out like flying chequer-boards. So the Bull gave orders for the undersides of our aircraft to be painted duck-egg blue, and this too was later adopted for all RAF fighters.

VI

BATTLE STATIONS

With the arrival of warm weather early in April the airfield, that had throughout the winter either been an inhospitable bog or covered with bleak, crackling ice, was transformed into a lush green veldt. We now practically lived there, having our meals delivered in the van and spending breaks between patrols basking in the welcome sun. But the days were drawing out, which meant long spells of Readiness.

Enemy tactics had recently shown an experimental tendency. All through the winter the German reconnaissance aircraft – the Dorniers, Heinkels and Ju 88s – had operated continuously but individually. They had paid particular attention to the area of the Ardennes and the Franco-Belgian frontier. Now these reconnaissance aircraft passed over the German frontier in squadron formation, breaking up over Thionville and dispersing on their various missions. The 109s had previously shown reluctance to cross the frontier or to engage our fighters. They had evidently maintained a standing patrol on their own side, only crossing to our side in small numbers and always very high. But now the German fighters came across in big formations: sometimes three squadrons of 109s would do a sweep as far as Metz and Nancy. The 110s had made their first appearance at the end of March, in close squadron formation and very high, only engaging when pressed into it by our Hurricanes. It was obvious that the Germans were practising offensive tactics, and it looked as though the bust-up might come soon.

This thought caused us to pay even more attention to our aircraft. Every pilot takes a pride in his own aeroplane, but the knowledge that he may be in action at any moment is naturally an additional incentive. There was now a marked increase of interest in the individual Hurricanes, and long hours were spent by ground crews and pilots in flight testing, altering rigging, adjusting control wires to the preferred tautness, tuning the engine, harmonizing the sights, checking the guns and testing them in the air, and generally getting everything on the top line.

For the benefit of the layman I should mention that the crew of a fighter does not consist solely of the pilot, although he is the only member who flies: the other two members, who are aircraftsmen, are just as vital; they are the fitter and the rigger. The fitter looks after the engine, the rigger the airframe. The pilot depends on these two men for his life. Normally the fitter and rigger take a personal pride in their pilot and would do anything for him. They are inextricably involved in his victories and defeats. Consequently there is a wonderful spirit of team-work and comradeship between the pilots, who are mostly officers, and the men – not only the fitters and riggers, but all the men in the various technical sections right down to the aircraft hands. My own fitter and rigger were two fine chaps, and much later, back in England, I paid a visit to my old squadron specially to thank them for the invaluable work they had done for me during the French campaign.

The sun shone cheerfully on 11 April and we were all on the airfield at mid-day hoping for some fun. A new French Bloch bomber* came in to show itself off to us. The pilot liked it and said it was Bloch's best production to date. It was no beauty, but seemed sturdy, and its performance figures were excellent. It had two engines and looked like a short, tubby Potez 63. A curious feature of the armament was an arrangement of three machine-guns placed underneath the observer, on fixed mountings, that had sufficient play to produce a spray. They pointed back and down – where an enemy fighter might line up below the tail – and were fired by the pilot. The observer had twin machine-guns on top and a respectable field of fire. We watched it take off and fly across the airfield as fast as a Hurricane.

Johnny was called to the telephone and came back with an incredulous look on his face. 'The Squadron's moving to Berry-au-Bac immediately!' he announced. We laughed – we'd been stuck so long

* The Bloch 174.

in one place that we'd forgotten we were supposed to be a mobile unit. 73 were already in the throes of a move (they might bloody-well have told us!) and we were to cover them, so all pilots had to stay on the airfield and leave the unfortunate batmen to do the private as well as the mess packing. By five o'clock the transport was trundling off and the Squadron was in the air in squadron forma-tion. It was very windy and the air was bumpy, and we did our best as we roared over Bar-le-Duc in a farewell salute. Our feelings were mixed as we wheeled away towards Reims. Some of us, perhaps, were wondering to what new ventures we were flying. But we all had heavy hearts as we realized that our happy days at Vassincourt and Bar-le-Duc had in a flash become a memory.

Berry-au-Bac airfield was thirty miles north-west of Reims on the main Reims–Laon road. In the north-west corner a Fairey Battle squadron was stationed. Our dispersal was along the south side, separated from a thick wood by unfenced fields. Two concrete huts constituted the pilots' room. Poking about in the wood we came across plenty of evidence of the Great War – old shell holes and trench systems, rusted unexploded shells, shrapnel scraps, and even a tree sniper's post with neat steps cut up the trunk.

Driving to the château which was to be our billet, we noted that the countryside in general still bore the ugly scars of battle. Torn, churned-up earth, fields discoloured and scarred by trenches and shell-holes, heaps of rusted metal and two war memorials, all testified to the death and destruction that had been here. The two memorials stood on high ground facing each other at a crossroads on the Reims–Laon road. One was a structure of granite blocks with a bronze knight's helmet set on the top, and inscribed 'AUX MORTS DES CHARS d'ASSAUT 1917'. The other was a plain granite crucifix, completely simple, but bearing an inscription so beautiful and so striking that I have never forgotten it:

'Ossements qu'animait un fier souffle naguère,
Membres épars, débris sans nom, humain chaos,
Pêle-mêle sacré d'un vaste reliquaire,
Dieu vous reconnaîtra, poussière de héros!' †

I thought of my father, who had spent four long years in the trenches in the First World War, and of the courage of the millions of fighting men who had given their lives between 1914 and 1918. In peacetime their sacrifice had been taken for granted and forgotten. But now that we stood on the ground on which they had fought and died we shared a common bond. We caught something of the atmosphere of the old British Expeditionary Force and the Royal Flying Corps. And we all felt, I think, that we had a fine tradition of bravery and endurance to live up to. For myself, throughout the French campaign, I was strongly conscious of the example – the presence beside me almost – of my father.

We were temporarily quartered at Guignicourt, a village four miles east of our airfield. 12 Squadron, who flew Battles, did their best to make us feel at home. On our first evening they threw an impromptu party, making sure we were never without a glass in our hands and flatly refusing to let us pay for anything. I was delighted to see one or two familiar faces among them: Eaton, Bill Simpson* and 'Judy' Garland (who not long afterwards earned a posthumous Victoria Cross). We were mutually interested in each others' work and swapped experiences. The bomber boys were horrified at the ungodly hour we were dragged out in the morning and at the peremptory way we were sent off on missions. We on our side didn't envy them their night flying and were amused by their 'Six-hour Readiness' – ours being five minutes.

We had already done a certain amount of liaison and cooperation with the Battles – practice attacks on them and so on – and we sympathized with them in their slow, under-armed machines. But they were pathetically confident in their tight formation with their fire-

---

* Soon to be shot down, have his life saved by the French and be repatriated by the Germans as one of the worst cases of burning ever to survive. Personality and sheer guts pulled him through, and he wrote three excellent books about his experiences.

---

†Heaps of bones once moved by the proud breath of life
Scattered limbs, nameless debris, chaos of humanity,
Sacred jumble of a vast reliquary,
Dust of heroes, God will know you!'

My poor translation cannot do the poetry justice, and in my ignorance I still do not know who wrote it.

concentration tactics. We admired their flying and guts, but although we gave them as much practice and encouragement as we could, we privately didn't give much for their chances.

A week later we moved our mess to Pontavert village, east of the airfield, where both pilots and troops were billeted. We made ourselves comfortable and settled down to make the most of the spring weather. Leak Crusoe, the adjutant, and I planned a dinner in Soissons, where there was an excellent restaurant. We were now quite resigned to the move and had quickly adjusted to our new and far-from-unpleasant surroundings. On 19 April, therefore, we were not amused when we arrived at the mess for lunch to find the indefatigable batmen packing up again and to learn we were returning to Vassincourt that afternoon.

Air Headquarters at Reims had applauded the precision of our formation as we flew over the town on arrival but deplored the publicity thus given to our movements. So this time we were to break up the Squadron twenty miles from Vassincourt and sneak discreetly into the airfield. Above all we were not to fly anywhere near Bar-le-Duc. It was obvious that this could only conceal our arrival by a couple of hours, but this might conceivably make a difference. There was a rash of foul oaths over the R/T as we approached the airfield one by one – we all came in so low we couldn't see each other until we were about to land. But we all made it safely.

I never discovered whether the move to our 'war station' at Berry-au-Bac was supposed to be an exercise or caused by genuine anticipation that the long-awaited German attack was imminent. Whichever it was, it must have provided some intriguing information for German air intelligence.

Anyway, we gaily announced our return to Madame Jean. True to her word, she laid on the promised Squadron dinner for the next evening – and what a feast it was! Through a thick fog I vaguely remember the proprietors of the Hôtel de Metz once more solemnly toasting the Squadron, and the Squadron equally solemnly toasting the proprietors of the Hôtel de Metz – with more than a passing feeling of affection for Madame Jean.

At the end of April we were told that the British 51st (Highland) Division was taking over the northern sector of the Maginot Line from the French and that an RAF Lysander army cooperation squadron had come down from the Pas-de-Calais to reconnoitre the sector for them. 87 Squadron had also come to give the Lysanders a Hurricane escort.

Naturally we wanted to welcome 87 to our terrain, to look them over and offer any information, help or advice they might need. So the Bull led a flight of us over to their airfield at Stenay, near 73 at Rouvres.

Conditions were extremely bumpy and we thought our formation over Stenay pretty ropey, but when we landed 87 congratulated us warmly. We'd heard they were a polite bunch! We spent a pleasant hour with them lolling about in deck chairs and savouring our drinks in the sun. I chattered away about old times with Michael Robinson, whom I was delighted to see again. We had been at Downside together and had become great friends since leaving. He had joined the RAF eighteen months ahead of me and had served in 111 Squadron, the first to get Hurricanes. He was just out from England to join 87 as a flight commander. We planned a combined celebration for our twenty-fourth birthdays the following week – mine was on 7 May and Micky's on 8 May.

But we never had that party. Micky took off in a Master on his birthday to join me at Vassincourt, ran into dirty weather and was forced down on a disused airfield. His brakes seized as he ran along the ground and the aircraft went over on its back. Fortunately it didn't catch fire, but Micky smashed his thumb badly and spent the remainder of the French campaign in hospital. A year later we were to fight together on Spitfires – but that is another story . . .

In spite of the general feeling of impending conflict, there was still time to appreciate the good things of life. The countryside was now in the full bloom of spring. Blossoming trees fringed the airfield; the grass took on a new rich greenness; the surrounding villages – Neuville, Revigny, Bussy – gleamed bright and clean in the sunlight; the barges on the canal, though always leisurely in pace, moved through the lock more frequently; and the river that flowed past our village was so fresh and clear that we began to select places to swim.

On 9 May Killy, Sammy Salmon (who had recently joined us) and I had a day off and decided to motor to Metz in the vintage Lagonda Sammy had wangled back – goodness knows how – from Malaya. He was not allowed to use it, so circumspection was the order of the day. We made a wide detour to avoid the main Bar-le-Duc road where one of our superior officers might just see us, and set course for Metz via St Mihiel to pick up a charming French girl called Germaine Demuth. She and her family were evacuees from Forbach on the German frontier.

We collected Germaine, who was delighted to see us, having few young friends in the district. It was a glorious sunny day and the breeze was warm and soft on our cheeks as we sped along at a comfortable sixty. At the top of the hill overlooking Metz we stopped to admire the fine city and the Moselle valley, the broad river curving away towards Germany.

We drove through the narrow streets of Metz to the main *Place*, exciting interest in our unusual carriage. We parked at a café and sat at a pavement table under a gaily striped awning. It was pleasant relaxing in the sun, sipping aperitifs and watching the passing parade: booted and spurred French Army officers, mostly escorting one of the many beautiful women of Metz; officer-pilots of the *Armée de l'Air* in dark-blue uniforms, some proudly wearing newly won *Croix de Guerre*; *Troupes de Forteresse* from the Maginot Line in black berets with their badges inscribed *'On ne passe pas!'* A giant of a man in the grey uniform of the Polish Air Force strode past powerfully and easily. He had that set expression, typical of the Poles, in which one sees the reflection of past sufferings and an implacable desire for victory.

In the late afternoon Killy and Sammy appointed a rendezvous where we would join up later and made off on their unlawful occasions. Germaine and I walked down to the famous old park and talked of many things. She told me of her family, of her friends now evacuees like herself, of the home in Forbach she never expected to see again. An RAF aircraftsman strolled down the path towards us, breaking into our reverie.

'Ah, an Englishman!' exclaimed Germaine.'You must speak to him.'

'No', I said, not welcoming the intrusion.

'Why not? Are you too proud?' she asked.

'No, no, on the contrary,' I mumbled. The fellow had a girl on his arm and I didn't want to embarass him. And I didn't want to catch a knowing look in *his* eye either.

'*Our* officers are always friendly with their men!' Germaine's voice was rising.

'So are ours, but sometimes it is bad for discipline.' I turned my head as the subject of the discussion passed by. I expect he grinned to himself; so did I.

'Oh – you English! You are just like the *Boches*!' We both laughed. Perhaps she was right.

The evening shadows were lengthening and the setting sun touched the turrets and spires of Metz with golden fingers. Gradually a faint sound disturbed our peace. We looked at each other. The sound came again, more distinct, but we were still not quite sure. The third time it was louder: a heavy rumbling, like distant thunder.

'*Les canons!*' Germaine said.

'Nonsense,' I tried to reassure her. 'It's only practice bombing. There are lots of ranges round here.'

It was the guns all right, big ones at that: the guns on the Maginot and Siegfried Lines. We walked back towards the town in silence, thinking our own thoughts.

VII
THE BUST-UP

I left Killy and Sammy on the *Mairie* steps when we got back to Neuville and took a stroll up to the airfield. It was a perfect night, with the stars bright and sharp. There were a lot of aircraft about and several passed over the village. The French anti-aircraft banged away furiously but, although they were lower than I'd ever heard them before, ineffectually.

It was noisy all night and I was restless. Several times I woke to the drone of aircraft and the sudden rending sound of ack-ack shells bursting low overhead. A nose-cap came whining through the air and hit the ground outside my window with a smack. I usually slept through minor manifestations of war, but tonight I tossed and turned, half-awake, half-dreaming. My dreams were of war, and the sounds of war in them constantly merged into the real sounds outside; there was something else too – a vague but haunting uneasiness that saddened me and made me feel afraid, as one feels in a nightmare . . .

I woke with a start to see the guard in my room. 'Wanted on the 'drome immediately, Sir!' he announced. Cursing, I rolled out and looked at my watch: three-thirty. It was already light. I dressed and dashed to the *Mairie*. 'What's up?' I asked Johnny. 'I've only been in bed two hours.'

' "B" Flight have already taken off,' Johnny answered curtly. I growled to myself. Then we were hanging all over the lorry that took us up to the airfield. Johnny rang Ops from the tent and came out laughing. 'Colledge [Wing's operations officer] is in one hell of a stew! He's got plots all over the board!'

At five came the order 'Patrol Metz angels 20.' We took off and soon were in formation climbing east. Thick haze persisted up to 5,000 feet, and although visibility above it was good, the ground was nearly invisible and the low sun made conditions worse. The only features of the landscape we could identify from our altitude were lakes and rivers, so finding the patrol line was a complicated business.

We didn't see any aircraft and had been droning up and down for forty minutes, fed-up and hoping 'B' Flight wouldn't have all the luck, when I heard over the R/T, very faintly and from another aircraft: 'Enemy aircraft going east from Ibor!' (Rouvres). 'Enemy aircraft going east from Ibor! Step on it for Christ's sake and get the bugger!' We all came-to with a jerk and closed in on Johnny, who swung away west.

Soon we saw it – a speck against the haze miles away to the right, lower than us and flying on a course parallel but in the opposite direction. We opened up to full throttle, black smoke pouring from our exhausts, and turned across the aircraft's path. He was still some way off when he saw us and dived north. We gave chase, still not quite certain of his identity.

'Line astern – Line astern – Go!' came Johnny's calm order over the R/T. Then as we drew nearer: 'Yes – I think so – yes-yes-yes – that's him! Number One Attack – Number One Attack – Go!'

Johnny was Number 1, Hilly was Number 2, I was Number 3. We watched Johnny go down on the diving Hun, his little Hurricane looking graceful but deadly. It was a Dornier 215, the new version of the 17. Johnny opened fire, but when his incendiaries were finished we couldn't see him firing. We saw him gradually close the range to about a hundred yards, then break away to the left and go down in a steep glide. Looks as though he's hit! Hilly got on to the Hun next, then it was my turn. We were now about 1,000 feet above the ground and the warm air was condensing on our cold windscreens, forming ice on the inside – we had been scrubbing like mad at them on the way down to clear them. I got in some good long bursts at close range, but the ice made things tricky, and to complicate the situation the Hun was now right on the deck, flying along valleys crammed with factory chimneys and skimming over thickly wooded hills. I made room for someone else and we attacked singly for another three minutes or so. The Hun pulled off some magnificent flying; it seemed rotten to have to smack him down. I had seen no fire from his rear gun – probably Johnny or Hilly had killed the rear gunner.

At last the Dornier reduced speed to such a degree that we had to zig-zag so as not to overshoot him. There were only three of us left – Hilly, Soper and myself – and we hauled off and watched him. Clearly he must crash or crash-land. He made a slow half-circuit round a field, straightened out, hit a ridge, bounced in the air, came down and slithered along the ground, knocking off panels and bits of engine cowling, and then came to rest.

We circled for five minutes, diving down to look at him. A posse of French soldiers ambled casually across from a nearby hamlet. As they approached, the roof of the Dornier's cockpit opened and a figure stood up, waving its arms at us as we circled overhead. The figure clambered on to the bullet-riddled wing and collapsed. The French completely ignored him, and fished down into the rear gunner's seat to pull something heavy out – doubtless the rear gunner. Hilly and I turned for home. Soper had gone. I had no clue as to where we were – I thought for a moment we were over Germany, as we could see miles of trenches – and I had no maps, so I stuck to Hilly like glue. A lot of aircraft were calling Rouvres for homing bearings and we couldn't get a word in edgeways. Hilly persevered and finally got a bearing. We arrived over Rouvres, where I landed for petrol. Hilly had plenty and went home.

While refuelling I had a chat with some of 73's boys. They had been busy too, having been rudely woken up by four Dorniers circling the airfield at dawn at the unprecedented height of 3,000 feet. It was 73's day off and they were all in bed, which was a pity to put it mildly. They took a decidedly poor view of those cheeky Dorniers, but in revenge later brought a Heinkel down close to the airfield. It exploded with such a roar that they reckoned it was carrying bombs. This was serious: if it was it meant the show was on. Certainly something was going on – there had been several formations about. Probably the Dorniers that circled Rouvres were looking for it and either couldn't identify it in the haze or were carrying out a reconnaissance.

Before leaving I admired the effect of a Hun bullet that had struck the bullet-proof section of a Hurricane's windscreen fair and square;

the windscreen was just a big star, far from transparent, but the bullet had only penetrated about a quarter of an inch before flattening out – a most comforting sight. Incidentally, Johnny *had* been hit in our fight and had force-landed near Rouvres with a bullet in the engine.

At Vassincourt, while refuelling, I met an *Armée de l'Air* officer I knew. He climbed up on my wing as I was about to taxi off and shouted: 'They have dropped bombs at Joinville, St Dizier and Châlons-sur-Marne – on the railway stations!' I shouted back: '*Les salauds!*' or something to that effect, adding that we had just shot one down. I waved goodbye, and taxiing over to the dispersal point wondered if his story was true. We heard such fantastic rumours . . . If it *was* true, then the bust-up we had been expecting for nine months had come. And yet there had been so many scares and false alarms, and nothing had happened for so long, that now we could scarcely believe it.

On getting back to the boys I learned that 'B' Flight had been in a fight. Prosser got a Dornier and Boy attacked another with such gusto that he only got in a short burst before over-shooting it and passing over the top. In doing so he presented a seductive target to the concentrated fire of all three Dorniers and got his aeroplane riddled with bullets for his trouble. One punctured a tyre and another came up through the floor, passing through the leg of his flying-boot and overalls and finishing up in the boost-pressure gauge. It was Boy we had heard calling the Hun's position.

Billy had spotted some 109s near Metz when he became separated from his section. Two attacked him, but pushed off after a bit of scrapping. Billy followed one flat-out and got near enough to open fire. The Hun dived to ground level and streaked off for Germany. Billy stuck to him well across the frontier. To shake him off the German flew under high-tension cables hoping to trap Billy into hitting them. Not to be outflown, Billy followed under, caught the Hun up and shot him down in flames in a wood, where he exploded. Nice work!

I was feeling very hungry and more than ready for lunch. I was therefore rather startled to find it was only nine o'clock. We'd been up since three-thirty and I felt as though we'd done a full morning's work already. But breakfast was as good as lunch and we all set to with a will when the van arrived. Afterwards we lay around in the sun sleeping it off.

Our orders now were only to intercept bombing raids that might interfere with 73's move to Reims-Champagne aerodrome. The French fighters were supposed to protect both their own air-fields and ours and to intercept all Hun bombers. Our next role was to cover the bombers of the Advanced Air Striking Force – the Battles and Blenheims – while they bombed the German Army's advance.

We waited three hours. There was nothing else to do except loll in the sun, which was now pretty savage. The batmen were packing our stuff down in the village. News came through that 87 Squadron's airfield had been bombed and that they had been in action. As most of them had not seen action before we wished them luck. 73 had been at it all morning and had bagged several enemy aircraft.

At about noon the telephone rang and we were ordered off for our first bombing cover: over the city of Luxembourg at 15,000 feet, to arrive at a stated time and to remain twenty minutes. 'B' Flight were detailed, but as one pilot was missing I asked to go. We had to take off immediately, as it was vitally important to synchronize our arrival over the target with that of the bombers. The Germans must be moving fast if they were in Luxembourg already, I thought.

Prosser was leading the show. The others were Boy, Billy, Lewis and Sergeants Berry and Albonico. I was designated 'Arse-end-Charlie'. Arse-end Charlie was the chap who hung about above and behind the formation, which was usually in open Vic. His job was to pro-tect the formation's tail, which was blind when flying straight, and to prevent surprise attack. We had learned this technique from the French soon after our arrival in eastern France, and usually had two 'Charlies', who proved indispensable. In fact, not once during the entire campaign was one of our formations surprised. We were often attacked from above, which is a different matter; but we always saw the enemy before he was in range and were never jumped.

We set off. The haze was now much thinner, and out of it rose thermally formed cumulus clouds. Being more or less detached from the formation, I could watch it as a whole from one side and above. The familiar sight of the Hurricanes now sent a thrill through me. There was something graceful yet deadly about them as they climbed, fast and straight as arrows, past the towering white clouds into the blue sky; something brave and resolute in their sharp-nosed flight to battle; and something not without beauty.

We arrived over the city on time. It lay clustered far below us, just visible between the clouds. We were too high to see any troop movements, and it looked much as when I had seen it, by accident, once before. We circled for the appointed twenty minutes, keeping our eyes well peeled, and then turned with some relief for home. We had expected a hot time of it, but hadn't seen a sausage. Then, somewhere near the Luxembourg border, we sighted a formation of fifteen Dorniers, in sections-line-astern and fine close formation; they must have been a first-rate squadron. We had trained ourselves to look above this sort of thing for trouble, and sure enough there it was – a squadron of 109s, split into two flights of six in aircraft-line-astern, one on each side of the bombers, 3,000 feet above and slightly behind them. Well played. We were in a hopelessly inferior position to attack the fighters, being level with the bombers, which had probably dropped their dirt, as they were travelling north-east If I had been leading the flight I would have tried to climb up to the fighters, probably with fatal consequences. But Prosser's experience told, and he called over the R/T: 'Leave them alone! Leave them alone! Do *not* attack!'

At the same moment we saw three other Hurricanes burst in on the scene. Without looking to left or right, or most important of all, above, they shot straight in behind the bombers. We watched the eerily fascinating spectacle as a flight of six 109s peeled off and came swooping down like hawks in line-astern. A second later a Hurricane burst into flames and went hurtling earthwards on its back. Christ! The bloody fools! The other two Hurricanes half-rolled smartly and beat it with everything they had. In a few seconds the 109s had regained their height, using the speed of their dive.

We had naturally approached flat-out to help when we saw the Hurricanes attacked. Now we were right underneath the German fighters, and both 109s and Hurricanes had broken up and were circling, they looking down at us waiting for us to make a pass at the Dorniers, and we looking up at them praying they wouldn't pounce, for they had all the height and outnumbered us two to one. But Prosser called 'Come on! Re-form! Re-form!' We obeyed smartly and dived away in good order, with me snaking about like mad behind. A neat well-drilled little trap, that! We never found out who the three rash Hurricanes belonged to, but they must have been from 73 or 87.

After the Luxembourg affair we were told to move once more to Berry-au-Bac. Wing had already left, and so had some of 'B' Flight. When 'A' Flight arrived at Vassincourt to hold the fort, the remainder of 'B' Flight pushed off. On the way they ran across some Heinkel 111s, Boy and Billy shooting down one each. Lewis, who was in another section, came across a Dornier and polished that off too.

Eventually we got the order to move. I flew in the Bull's section. We were soon over Berry, having noticed the results of heavy bombing on the way. As we circled the airfield we saw a collection of bomb craters where several sticks of anti-personnel bombs ('That means you!' I thought with a shock) had fallen among the Battles. We landed at four, parked our aircraft and ambled over to the concrete hut where the boys were gathered.

We were feeling very weary by now, and as some of us had not eaten since nine o'clock we were bloody famished. I sprawled out with my head on a pile of gravel underneath some larch trees. We had to hang around in case we were suddenly ordered off, though how this was to be done no one knew – the telephone to Wing was not yet connected and the petrol tankers had not arrived to refuel our aircraft.

I lay on the ground relaxing gratefully, stretched out in dirty overalls and flying boots with my hands supporting my head, my parachute and helmet beside me in case they should be needed in a hurry. It was oppressively hot. The slender branches of the trees above me were laden with May bugs and the little beasts kept dropping on me. In the distance was the boom of continuous bombing.

I wondered how 73 were doing; their aerodrome at Reims-Champagne had been bombed before their arrival, and all the dummy Hurricanes (mocked-up to deceive German reconnaissance) were destroyed in a hangar. Rather a joke, we thought. The booms got louder. War over France . . .

By contrast, an old peasant was tilling his land a hundred yards away with a horse-drawn harrow. A youth – his son perhaps – was following him up and down the newly raked field. Two other farmhands were harrowing behind a fine team of horses in the same field. I had recently taken some shots of them and promised to give them a print, but hadn't yet had the opportunity to develop the negatives.

I dozed, somehow reassured by this pastoral scene in spite of the sound effects of war off. The sound of bombing got suddenly louder and the drone of aircraft woke me up. The boys were peering up and I jumped up to join the squinting party. The sky was almost clear, with just a few little puffs of cloud.

'There they are! They're turning!' said Prosser. Yes, there they were! About twenty bombers – Heinkels by the look of them – turning east. But one didn't.

'What's that mug up to?' said Leslie.

We watched. He was flying straight over us.

'He's doing a bombing run – yes! See him correct then?' I answered indifferently, remembering the days I used to drop practice bombs from an Overstrand.

'Balls! Anyway, you won't see me budge if he drops a bomb right there!' Leslie waved casually at the ground thirty yards away.

We craned our necks anxiously as the Hun disappeared behind a small cloud. Then we heard it – first a whisper, then a faint whistle that rose to an unearthly shriek that filled and split the heavens as if all the devils in hell had been let loose. A swift glance at each other, a shocked look of realization on our faces, a few frantic stumbling paces towards the concrete hut – then flat on our faces in the dust as the bombs burst with a series of shattering, drum-splitting, terrifying crashes. I was beside a lorry, cringing as the huge tyres bounced off the ground with each bang. Fragments pattered against it, against the hut, all around us. Then – stillness.

No one moved. I raised my head cautiously, expecting a scene of death and desolation. But no – all the boys were there, thank God, each raising a dazed head. Leslie laughed raucously and we all jumped up grinning and wiping the sweat from our faces.

'Quite close, those!' remarked the Bull casually. 'Funny, I've never seen Boy and Paul look so small!' More laughter.

'Crummy bloody bastard!' roared Leslie, summing up our feelings as usual. 'What wouldn't I give to get that sod!'

Hilly was quiet. 'Legitimate military objective,' he muttered. He was right, of course. And the difference of a hair's breadth and a split second to that German bomb-aimer would have wiped out No 1 Squadron . . .

A faint shout from the field behind made us turn. We saw one of the young farmhands staggering towards us. We ran over to him. His face was black with mud, dust and powder; his clothes ripped and dishevelled; he was all-in. The bombs had fallen all round him – how he escaped I don't know. We supported him as he pointed across the field, distraught.

'Ils sont morts! Tous les trois! Ils sont là-bas!' We looked across and saw an indistinct heap near the wood. The bombs had dropped in two sticks – fourteen of them – starting on the fringe of the wood and extending to thirty yards from where we had lain.

We found them among the craters. The old man lay facedown, his body twisted grotesquely, one leg shattered and a savage gash across the back of his neck oozing steadily into the earth. His son lay close by, in a state I will not describe. Against the hedge I found what must have been the remains of the third boy – recognizable only by a few tattered rags, a broken boot and some splinters of bone. The five stricken horses lay bleeding beside the smashed harrows; we shot them later. The air was foul with the reek of high-explosive, and the bomber that had laid these poisonous eggs was scarcely out of sight, so quick had the raid been. The boy with us threw out his arms to embrace the scene, as if trying to comprehend it. He pointed to the old man and choked: *'Et lui le père de huit enfants . . .'* He spun round, violently shaking his fist in the air at the departing raider, and shouted passionately *'Oui, je te casse' la gueule, toi!'*

I imagined the German bomb-aimer, headed for his base at 18,000 feet, entering in his log: 'Military objective bombed Berry-au-Bac: British airfield. Hits – no damage observed.' And the experts who would later examine the photographs would just note a line of bursts, starting in a wood and ending beside a concrete hut . . .

That evening I flew two more patrols – one over the airfield and another over Reims. Smoke was rising from several towns and villages: bombed. Reims-Champagne aerodrome was a patchwork of vari-coloured craters: poor old 73 had had the full treatment. Here and there farmhouses and barns were burning, and the sight of the lazy red flames licking up nauseated me: it was all so thoroughly evil and hellish.

We landed in the evening, and though there was still an hour or two of daylight left, the Bull thought we'd had enough for one day. So we piled into the bus and drove away, past the dead horses, past the sombre crucifix at the crossroads, down to Pontavert. We were tired, hungry and strung-up. My head had scarcely touched the pillow when I was asleep, having barely summoned the energy to say a prayer. So ended 10 May, 1940 – our first day of real war.

VIII
ACTION

We were up again at two forty-five AM, refreshed by a short but sound sleep. We had to be on the airfield half an hour before dawn, but grabbed a biscuit and a cup of tea in the mess first.

The Bull decided that our concrete pilots' hut was too obvious a target. We guessed the German bomber had been aiming at it the previous evening, and considering he was flying at 18,000 feet* his bombing had been damned accurate. Accordingly the Bull chose a spot some 250 yards away on the fringe of the wood, and we spent the first hours of daylight rigging up a tent into which we moved the telephone to Wing, a couple of desks and our flying kit. There was a shallow trench and dug-out nearby that looked as though they might be useful. They were . . .

We climbed into our cockpits at eight as there was a hell of a lot of bombing going on. We sat ready and strapped in, gazing into the sky to the east, with an aircraftsman sitting beside each plugged-in starter battery. The scheme was to get the aircraft off the ground and out of harm's way if there was a raid, and perhaps to knock down a few bombers – although this was not our primary job. In this particular case 'B' Flight were ordered to get off first and chase the Huns, with 'A' Flight to follow and circle the airfield, or engage if there was a chance.

My aircraftsman suddenly stood up and peered at the sky behind me. I had my helmet on and couldn't hear much, but I could pick

---

* This height was confirmed much later for me by Captain Michael Worthington, Royal Artillery, whose 3.5 inch anti-aircraft guns fired on the Heinkel.

up a lot of crumps going off. I twisted round as far as my straps would let me and looked up. Yes, there was something up there all right! Shells from the British ack-ack battery were bursting all over the place. A 'B' Flight engine sprang to life at the other end of the line. I waved to the aircraftsman and in a moment my prop was whirling in front of me and the machine vibrating. As I waited for 'B' Flight to get off I watched engine after engine start up; and in a minute the first 'B' Flight aircraft roared off across our noses, followed in quick succession by the other five. I looked up right as the aircraftsman waggled my aileron and pointed. Yes! There were the buggers, turning away east at a good 15,000 feet.

Soon I too was off. No time to lose, no time to join up even, and I started climbing flat-out beside two 'B' Flight aircraft – one of them with Billy's 'P' on its side – after the raiders. They must have seen us take off, and we thought later we had probably foiled a heavy attack on the airfield, for they were now climbing at full throttle dead into the sun: good tactics. They were Heinkels – about twelve – in very open formation, probably because they were flat-out. We were catching them slowly, but it became apparent that if we ever made it we would probably be over Berlin. One of the 'B' Flight Hurricanes rolled over and dived away for home in what must have been disappointed disgust. Billy kept on. It was obvious there wasn't much hope now, so I looked around for something, maybe, within reach.

I found it – about five miles away to the right and below me. I couldn't see what it was, but it stood out clearly against the top of the haze, and as I turned sharply towards it, it gave the clue to its nationality by turning from its westerly course and diving steeply east, evidently having seen me too. I nearly lost it in the haze, but soon got nearer and saw it was a Dornier 215. Having made quite sure, I attacked from astern. The fellow was moving bloody fast and it was all I could do in my slow old wooden-blader to get within range. Long before I did so the Hun rear gunner betrayed his feelings by loosing off wildly, the tracers flashing past me all over the place. I fired a short preliminary burst at long range, partly to put him off and partly to steady my aim, and having closed and got my sights on, I opened fire.

The German started turning, first one way, then the other. The rear gunner stopped firing. Realizing that once he was on the deck any shooting would be difficult, I fired longish bursts following each other as rapidly as possible. Soon he was right down on the trees, slowing but still travelling fast. Each time I fired I saw whitish smoke pump from one engine or the other – doubtless glycol – but the determined bloody man kept right on flying. I ran out of ammunition, but must have hit his oil system as my windscreen was spattered with black oil.

I pulled off and watched him from above. Still no fire from the rear gun, but something glowing like a Verey light floated up towards me; I thought at the time it was a defiant shot from the Hun's Verey pistol, his gun being jammed, but decided later it was probably a French tracer shell from the ground. Anyway, as soon as he saw I'd stopped attacking he turned half-right and flew straight due east. I did a roll over the top of him to wish him luck and left, as he showed no signs of coming down now and I didn't know where I was. If his engines lasted long enough without glycol and oil he probably made it all right, and I rather hope he did. Either my shooting was bloody poor or he was loaded with armour, or both. But I felt he'd got the best of me, so I metaphorically raised my hat to him and departed.

I circled uneasily for a few minutes trying to pick up my bearings. The country was thickly wooded and green. Luxembourg? Belgium? Somewhere round there, I thought. As usual my luck held. I came to an airfield with Potez 63s parked round the edge and honeycombed with bomb craters varying in diameter from six feet to sixty. I was in the right country, but short of fuel, so I landed. In trying to dodge one of the smaller bomb holes, which were invisible at a distance, I swerved violently and dug my port wing in, bending the tip.

I taxied over, wondering what the hell I was going to do about dear old 'G', my aeroplane. The airfield was Mézières. I dug out the French squadron CO, who got an engineer to look my Hurricane over. The engineer said it definitely could not fly, as engineers will. The ailerons still worked, though, and I thought it would fly with full right aileron. The CO left the decision to me but emphasized that he wouldn't fly it. He thought it would misbehave coming in to land. As he was a pilot of some twenty-five years' experience I decided to follow his advice.

The French CO was a tall, hard-looking man, bursting with

efficiency and quite undisturbed by the numerous delayed action bombs scattered about the airfield. 'Oh, those!' he said contemptuously, 'they've been going off all night. One gets used to anything in time . . .'

His squadron was engaged in bombing and reconnaissance, operating with the French light mechanized units which had advanced into Luxembourg and southern Belgium. They had not suffered many losses yet. 'But,' he added despondently, 'if *only* we had more fighters . . .'

He very decently put an aircraft at my disposal to fly me back to Berry, and having taken my maps and parachute out, I said *au revoir* to poor old 'G' with her gay red spinner. It was to be goodbye, but I still feel sentimental about her. Three days later Sammy took a lorry and a party of riggers to Mézières to patch her up and bring her home. He was only there five minutes when there was a whine and a roar from the sky, whereupon he was compelled to recline in a ditch for two and a half hours while the airfield was wholeheartedly strafed by low-flying Dorniers. Sammy said he could actually see the pilots and gunners as they flew up and down a matter of yards away bombing and machine-gunning. They did their stuff beautifully, setting fire to all fifteen Potez and an assortment of other aircraft and leaving the place a write-off. Sammy's lorry was shot up. But, worst news of all to me, poor old 'G' was sieved with bullets. I can only hope she burned before the Huns laid their rude hands on her.

During the trip back I spent most of the time fiddling about with the machine-gun in the rear cockpit. The aeroplane was a Mureau – a pretty old open parasol monoplane with a Hispano engine; it looked like a First World War effort. The pilot kept glancing round anxiously to see what I was playing at, while I was hoping no German fighters would appear, at any rate until I'd got the gun working. A fat lot of use it would have been anyway.

Back with the Squadron, I didn't claim the Dornier, but entered it as a 'possible' in my log book. Wing had kicked up a fuss about our taking off to chase up bombing raids, and AHQ at Reims pointed out curtly that since we were there primarily to provide cover for our bombers on their missions, how the blazes could we rush off all over the sky every time we saw an enemy bomber? We were *not* – repeat *not* – to take off without orders. If a bombing raid came over we were to lie down and lump it. All very fine for them deep down in their champagne-cellar shelters. But we supposed they were right; they sometimes were. However, we learnt with relish that three jumbo bombs had dropped just outside their Reims château, wiping out some transport and frightening the pants off them. 'What did they expect, setting up their HQ in a perfect target?' said Prosser tartly.

That same afternoon we were ordered to patrol AHQ at Reims! We were up an hour and a half but saw nothing. I believe the chaps at Headquarters felt a little more confident seeing us droning about over the city. Reims had been bombed, but I couldn't see any damage. I hoped to God the Germans wouldn't knock the cathedral down again; the restorers had only just finished making good the World War I damage.

Back at the airfield, 'A' Flight dashed off to Pontavert for tea. I had eaten nothing that day and had been up since before three, so I wasn't sorry. We swallowed the hot tea and bread-and-jam, then rushed back to the airfield as a message came through from Wing that a big formation of bombers was heading for Reims – forty-five, they said!

As I doubled across to my new aircraft I met Squadron Leader White, the Roman Catholic padre to the local Battle squadrons. I had met him on our previous visit to Berry in April and thought him a damn good chap. He asked me if I wanted absolution, puffing along beside me. I confessed briefly. He asked if there were any other Catholics who might want absolution. I said 'Only old Killy in that Hurricane over there – he hasn't wanted it for ten years, but you can try!' We laughed and I waved him goodbye. But confess Killy did – sitting in his cockpit with the padre standing on the wing beside him. He was a good man, that padre. I never saw him again.

Five minutes later we were off. 'Patrol Panther [AHQ Reims] angels 10' came over the R/T. Up we climbed – Johnny leading, Hilly No 2 on his right, myself No 3 on the left, and Killy and Soper 4 and 5 respectively and doing the cross-over behind. After fifteen minutes over Reims we were called up: 'Two enemy aircraft going west from Sedan – two Dorniers going west – angels 5.' We closed in and shot off north, rubbing our hands at the thought of only two Dorniers to five Hurricanes at 5,000 feet.

Approaching Sedan Johnny called: 'There they are! There they are! Straight ahead!' I couldn't see them at first, but suddenly I did, and my heart leapt. As we got nearer I counted them – thirty Dorniers in two squadrons of fifteen more or less in line abreast, covered by fifteen 110s in groups of twos and threes wheeling and zig-zagging slowly above, ahead, beside and behind the bombers. They were going west across our noses from right to left.

Johnny rocked his wings for us to close in tighter and pressed straight on, climbing a little to 7,000 feet, then turning left and diving at the Huns from astern. 'Now keep in – keep in – and keep a bloody good look-out!' he said steadily. I was swivel-eyed as we approached, to make sure we were not being attacked by something unseen, for the Huns continued straight on although we were closing on them. They must have seen us long before, but it was not until the last moment that the 110s wheeled, some to the right and some to the left, going into aircraft-line-astern in twos and threes.

We went in fast in a tight bunch, each picking a 110 and manoeuvring to get on his tail. I selected the rear one of two in line-astern who were turning tightly to the left. He broke away from his No 1 when he had done a half-circle and steepened his turn, but I easily turned inside him, holding my fire until I was within fifty yards and then firing a shortish burst at three-quarters deflection. To my surprise a mass of bits flew off him – pieces of engine-cowling and lumps of his glasshouse (hood) – and as I passed just over the top of him, still in a left-hand turn, I watched with a kind of fascinated horror as he went into a spin, smoke pouring out of him. I remember saying 'My God, how ghastly!' as his tail suddenly swivelled sideways and tore off, while flames streamed over the fuselage. Then I saw a little white parachute open beside it. Good!

Scarcely half a minute had passed, yet as I looked quickly around me I saw four more 110s go down – one with its tail off, a second in a spin, a third vertically in flames, and a fourth going up at forty-five degrees in a left-hand stall-turn with a little Hurricane on its tail firing into its side, from which burst a series of flashes and long shooting red flames. I shall never forget it.

All the 110s at my level were hotly engaged, so I searched above. 'Yes – those buggers up there will be a nuisance soon!' Three cunning chaps were out of the fight, climbing like mad in line-astern to get above us to pounce. I had plenty of ammunition left, so I climbed after them with the boost-override pulled. They were in a slight right-hand turn, and as I climbed I looked around. There were three others over on the right coming towards me, but they were below. I reached the rear 110 of the three above me. He caught fire after a couple of bursts and dived in flames. Then I dived at the trinity coming up from the right and fired a quick burst at the leader head-on.

I turned, but they were still there; so were the other two from above. In a moment I was in the centre of what seemed a stack of 110s, although there were in fact only five. I knew I had scarcely the speed or height in my wooden-blader to dive away and beat it, so I decided to stay and make the best of it. Although I was more manoeuvrable at this height than the Huns, I found it impossible to get in an astern shot because every time I almost got one lined up tracers came whipping past from another on my tail. All I could do was to keep twisting and turning, and when a 110 got behind me make as tight a turn as possible, almost spinning with full engine, and fly straight at him, fire a quick burst, then push the stick forward and dive under his nose. I would then pull up in a steep climbing turn to meet the next gentleman.

Obviously they couldn't all attack at once without colliding, but several times I was at the apex of a cone formed by the cannon and machine-gun fire of three of them. Their tactics consisted mostly of diving, climbing and taking full deflection shots at me. Their shooting seemed wild. This manoeuvre was easily dealt with by turning towards them and popping over their heads, forcing them to steepen their climb until they stalled and had to fall away. But I was not enjoying this marathon. Far from it. My mouth was getting drier and drier, and I was feeling more and more desperate and exhausted. Would they run out of ammunition? Would they push off? Would help come? I knew I couldn't hold out much longer.

After what seemed an age (actually it turned out to be at least fifteen minutes, which is an exceptionally long time for a dogfight) I was flying down head-on at a 110 which was climbing up to me. We both fired – and I thought I had left it too late and we would collide. I pushed the stick forward violently. There was a stunning explosion right in front of me. For an instant my mind went blank. My aircraft seemed to be falling, limp on the controls. Then, as black smoke poured out of the nose and enveloped the hood, and a hot blast and a flicker of reflected flame crept into the dark cockpit, I said 'Come on – out you go!', pulled the pin out of my harness, wrenched open the hood and hauled myself head-first out to the right.

The wind pressed me tightly against the side of the aircraft, my legs still inside. I caught hold of the trailing edge of the wing and heaved myself out. As I fell free and somersaulted I felt as if a giant had me on the end of a length of wire, whirling me round and round through the air. I fumbled for and pulled the rip-cord and was pulled the right way up with a violent jerk that winded me. My head was pressed forward by the parachute back-pad that had slipped up behind, and I couldn't look up to see if the parachute was OK. I had no sensation of movement – just a slight breeze as I swung gently to and fro. For all I knew the thing might be on fire or not properly open.

I heard the whirr of Hun engines and saw three of the 110s circle me. I looked at the ground and saw a shower of flaming sparks as something exploded in an orchard far below: my late aeroplane.

The Hun engines faded and died. I rolled the ripcord round its D-ring and put it in my pocket as a souvenir. I was still bloody frightened, as I was smack over a wood and thought I'd probably break my legs if I landed in it; and I confess without shame that I reeled off several prayers, both of thanks and supplication, as I dangled in the air. I was soon low enough to see my drift. It was towards a village, and it looked as though I might clear the trees only to hit a roof. But no – it was to be the wood all right. I was very low now, swinging gently. I saw two French gendarmes running along the road, first one way, then the other. I waved to them. The trees rushed up at me. Now for it! I relaxed completely, shutting my eyes calmly. There was a swish of branches and a bump as I did a back-somersault on the ground. I had fallen between the trees.

I jumped up as the two gendarmes came crashing through the trees, one with a revolver in his hand and the other carrying a rifle. *'Haut les mains!'* they shouted, pointing their weapons at me. I raised my arms as they advanced cautiously. I was wearing white overalls over my uniform and still had my helmet and oxygen mask on. I spoke through the mask with difficulty and they refused to believe

I was English, but I eventually managed to persuade them to look for the RAF wings under my overalls. Having done this, they put down their weapons and embraced me warmly.

I tore off my helmet and threw it on the ground, shouting *'Ces salauds de Boches!'* which relieved my feelings slightly. We gathered up my parachute and moved on to the village. I rode in the side-car of their motorcycle combination. The entire population of Rumigny had witnessed the fight and had seen six Huns come down nearby; they later found four more, making a total of ten. They had watched me fighting the remaining five and said it had lasted at least fifteen minutes, perhaps more.*

When I got back to the Squadron I found that Johnny claimed to have shot down one definitely, and perhaps two, Hilly two, Killy two and Soper two. With my two that made exactly the number found – ten – leaving the number I had fought as five (total fifteen as counted before the fight). The villagers on the ground had seen two enemy tails come off – presumably one was mine; the other was Killy's. The police presented me with one of the fins; with the black-and-white swastika pierced by two bullets, it made a respectable match for the two First War fins we had with the Black Cross emblems on them.

Donald Hills, our equipment officer, came over to collect me in the Renault, but as it was late we decided to stay the night. We ate and drank well. The French were enthusiastic over our victory, and I was encouraged to hear that the thirty Dorniers had turned and beetled off when we tackled their fighter escort. The French had taken prisoner the pilot of the first 110 to crash, which had been mine, and we rang up during dinner to find out if we could see him. He had a bullet in the thigh and was in hospital When we got through he had just been taken away by French air intelligence, but an officer who had spoken to him gave us some details; he was twenty-three, a fanatical Austrian Nazi from Vienna, and said he was furious to be knocked out of the war so soon. He must have been a liar too, for he claimed to have shot me down. As I went down a good fifteen minutes later, long after his departure, I thought his claim a trifle extravagant.†

There was only one bed available, so Donald and I had to share

---

*One man based his estimate on the time it took him to walk a distance he knew well, which he did during the fight.

it. We'd wined and dined too well to care. Before dinner I had tramped a good seven miles across country looking for one of the Huns, led by a tough little *Chasseur*, so I was extremely tired.

We woke up in the grey dawn to the reverberations of very heavy bombing: Liart and Hirson, two neighbouring towns with railway junctions, were being flattened, with a big civilian death toll. As one of the Frenchmen had said to me at dinner, *'Il est fort, ce Boche!'*

We got back to the Squadron at tea-time on 12 May, displaying my fin in triumph. Killy told me he had seen me stuck with the Huns but could only say 'Poor bastard!' to himself and buzz off, as he had no ammunition left, and neither had anyone else. It was my own fault for getting stuck anyway.

The airfield had been bombed twice during my absence. 'B' Flight had been at it again – Leslie Clisby got two Dornier 17s at Avaux, where he had landed on the airfield and been shot up by the French ground defences doing so. Prosser and Boy each got a 110 in the fight.

†The French gendarmerie verified on the spot the German losses in this fight and reported them to me personally in the presence of Donald Hills as well as through normal channels. On 30 June German records reported two Me 110s lost on 11 May near Hirson and nothing more. It appears that our fight was with Z.G. 26 'Horst Wessel', and this may be the reason why a fight in which they lost two-thirds of their number to one-third their number of Hurricanes was not recorded. In any case, the accuracy of German reports of their losses must clearly be called in question.

IX
REACTION

At this stage I began to feel peculiar. I had a hell of a headache and was jumpy and snappy. Often I dared not speak for fear of bursting into tears. I thought the explosion (probably a cannon shell in the front petrol tank) had concussed me slightly, as I had the familar concussion symptoms. I was sitting on the verandah steps with Boy and Prosser when Boy said: 'Come on Paul, give us the big story!' I surprised myself and them by snapping 'Oh shut up! Who the hell cares?' and striding off, leaving the two of them staring after me. But Boy came across as I was moodily kicking the verandah rails and said: 'This isn't like you, Paul. You'd better have a word with Doc. He'll sort you out in no time.' 'I'm OK,' I muttered, 'probably got slight concussion.' But Boy persisted, and I finally saw Doc Brown. He immediately ordered me off to bed for twenty-four hours, and he wasn't a man to trifle with. 'I'll straighten it out with the CO, and bring you some dope to make you sleep,' he said kindly. Thank God we had our Doc. He looked after us devotedly and saved us many breakdowns.

Before I left the mess I heard that some of the boys were going to Holland that evening to do a cover for our bombers over Maastricht. I was relieved that I wasn't going – I didn't feel I could take it just at that moment.

As I walked up the sunny, dusty street to my billet, I looked through aching eyes at the little war memorial inscribed 'PONTAVERT A SES MORTS GLORIEUX'. The sound of intermittent bombing beat on my ears, my head was splitting, my emotions almost beyond control. I looked up into the brazen sky and wondered if I could hang on, and if so, for how long?

At my billet I met the old lady who owned the house. She was very happy to see me again, having feared the worst. I told her I had escaped by parachute, and she said fervently, *'Vous êtes destiné à vivre!'* I wasn't convinced.

In my room I sponged myself down with cold water. It was a relief to get the dust, oil and sweat of three days off my body. I closed the shutters and lay down, but couldn't sleep. That blasted bombing had me listening to it. Every time the ack-ack guns behind the airfield banged off I jumped up and threw open the shutters. I watched the white shell-bursts against the blue evening sky, and saw a Ju 88 dive-bomb the airfield with heavy bombs; Prosser and some of the other pilots were in the dug-out and didn't like it, I later heard: the bombs fell very close. Doc Brown arrived and gave me a couple of pills. After some time I slept.

Scarcely had I dropped off when I was in my Hurricane rushing head-on at a 110. Just as we were about to collide I woke up with a jerk that nearly threw me out of bed. I was in a cold sweat, my heart banging wildly. I dropped off again – but the nightmare returned. This went on at intervals of about ten minutes all night. I shall never forget how I clung to the bed-rail in a dead funk. If there is ever a choice between physical and mental pain, I'll take physical every time.

At dawn I fell into a deep sleep, and slept through two more bombing raids on the airfield. I got up – at five on the evening of 13 May – and walked to the mess feeling rested, but weak and unreal, as if in a trance.

X
PILOTE ANGLAIS?

There was plenty of news. The Maastricht show had been a hot affair. The Bull had crash-landed in Belgium and was missing; Lewis had baled out on the wrong side of the lines and was probably a prisoner of war; Hilly's aircraft had stopped two cannon shells, but he had got back all right; Leslie had knocked off two Arados* and a 109, Killy a Heinkel 112†, and Soper, Laurie and Peter Boot (recently joined) a 109 each. It was later confirmed that the Bull had got a 109 and an Arado*, and Lewis a 109 and possibly a second.

(It was in this action that five Battles of 12 Squadron bombed the Maas bridges. 'Judy' Garland, the leader, was awarded a posthumous VC. All five Battles were shot down and only two aircrew out of fifteen escaped alive. The bridges were reported hit. Volunteers had been called for to take part in the raid and, of course, the whole of 12 Squadron had stepped forward.)

A short time after I was told all this the Bull rolled up unheralded in a Belgian car. He had crash-landed with his engine riddled with bullets. He had witnessed some rough scenes in Belgium, among which he described four regiments of French Senegalese troops proceeding to the front at the trot, looking neither to right nor left, with implacable expressions on their faces. A Heinkel crash-landed in a field beside the road, and a section of Senegalese doubled across to it, dragged the German crew of four out and promptly decapitated them

---

* At this time we habitually mis-identified the Henschel Hs 126 army co-operation aircraft.

† Presumably, though not certainly, a mis-identification: Killy was a very experienced pilot.

on the spot. They then resumed their progress, without a word or even a change of expression.

That same day – 13 May – 'B' Flight had been on the chase when Billy had called something about oxygen over the R/T and left the formation. Nothing had been heard of him since, and it didn't look too good.

As we stood chatting desultorily in the mess garden at twilight we heard some crumps not far away. The airfield again? A few minutes later we heard aeroplane engines and were surprised to see a French machine of some sort – a twin with twin rudders – flying low over the tree-tops past the village.

'He's on the run from something,' Killy said, 'and asking to be blown out of the sky, flying like that!' As the aircraft passed by with a roar we looked at each other, mystified.

'Stone the flaming crows!' said Leslie. 'If that wasn't a bloody Dornier I'll eat my epaulettes!'

'With French markings – the bastard!' Johnny snorted.

'That means we'll be bombed tomorrow, boys,' said the Bull.

'Well bugger me! Let's have another drink.' That of course was from Prosser.

We proceeded to do just that when an old peasant rushed into the garden. Moses Demozay, our interpreter, took charge of him. In a flood of French he told Moses that he had seen a series of red Verey lights fired along the ground towards the village from a copse as the disguised Dornier had flown over. We emptied our tankards with a gulp, grabbed our revolvers and a couple of our German machine-guns, piled into and all over the Bull's brake and roared over to the copse indicated by the old man. We surrounded and combed it thoroughly, but found nothing. I expect whoever had fired the lights was miles away by that time. Perhaps it was the old boy who told us!

That night we had a grim assortment of warnings from AHQ about a parachute invasion. It was believed airborne troops would attempt to seize our airfield and bump us off in the village. The Bull immediately reorganized the airfield defences and ordered us all to sleep armed in the mess. He informed us, the troops and the villagers that anyone seen off the roads between dusk and dawn would be shot on sight.

During dinner the Bull was called to the telephone and came back beaming. He said that Lewis had been taken prisoner by the Germans but had been rescued in a Belgian counter-attack. A cheer went up. Lewis was now on his way to Maubeuge to await our transport.

After dinner the Bull called me aside and said: 'Look here Paul, I want Lew picked up as soon as possible. Moses is needed here and you're the only one who speaks French decently, so take the Renault with Owens as driver and push off as soon as possible.' I thought 'Bloody hell!' but said 'Righto, Sir' and rushed out to call Owens. It was ten-thirty by the time we got going, and nearly dark. Refugees were beginning to stream through our village, but after dark the traffic slackened.

'The last time you drove me in this thing we went to Nancy, Owens. Do you remember?'

'I do, Sir! You, Mr Walker, Mr Kilmartin, Mr Crusoe and Mr Salmon. *Those* were the days, Sir! A bit different now!'

'Very. I wonder how old Nancy's looking. I hear it's been heavily bombed and they've had a lot of civilians killed. Hit the hospital – but it was close to the airfield . . . Metz has been *shelled* too. Poor old Metz! They've bombed St Dizier, Revigny, Châlons, Vitry – all our old favourite towns . . .'

From these melancholy thoughts I passed to a contemplation of the German plan. I could not hate the Germans, in spite of the devastation they were spreading. So far they appeared to have stuck strictly to military objectives. We heard horror stories, of course – towns flattened out, hospitals bombed indiscriminately, refugees machine-gunned. But the Germans are by nature thorough, and war is essentially brutal. We felt they still held a full hand of excuses for accidents caused during raids on legitimate military objectives. In the air, too, they had so far fought like gentlemen. I remembered dangling helplessly in my parachute while the 110s buzzed round me and, though it didn't enter my head at the time, I have since always been grateful they let me go. No, the *Luftwaffe* had been playing the game, and it was certainly having the game all its own way. But when the Hun is checked, I thought, then watch it! Once the tide turns slightly against him he'll strip off the kid gloves.

We had just passed through Guignicourt and it was now dark. We were forbidden to use headlights, but with the chaos of unlighted cars, carts and assorted obstructions on the road it was dangerous without them. Suddenly we picked up a figure in our headlight beams standing in the middle of the road waving its arms. It was a French army officer wearing one of their small new helmets. There was a lot of fifth-column funny business going on, so I took out my automatic and nursed it in my lap. We stopped as the little Frenchman came running over. I was more suspicious when I saw the state he was in.

'*Oh monsieur! Monsieur!* An accident – a terrible accident has occurred.' The man was weeping and hamming it up, and I was convinced something definitely fishy was going on. I asked for his identity card.

'*Oui, mon cher monsieur!* Quite right, *monsieur!*' he said, producing it. We took him on board and drove to his car, which had dim lights and the front bashed in. A motorcycle was overturned nearby.

'We had no lights!' exclaimed the Frenchman, weeping all over the place. I still feared a trap. Two other French officers were there.

'Where's the motor-cyclist?' I asked.

'Ah, over there somewhere . . .' The Frenchman waved vaguely.

I went across and found a British dispatch-rider from the Royal Corps of Signals lying with his head in a pool of blood. His dispatches were still slung and seemed intact. He was alive. We lifted him into the van, and I sat in the back with his head in my hands while Owens drove. We returned to Guignicourt and got hold of 12 Squadron's doctor, whom I knew. He took charge of the man – who was just coming round – and we rushed on at top speed. I scarcely had time to wipe the blood from my hands on the grass. I never heard what happened to our dispatch-rider, although Doc Brown told me he thought he had died. I hope not.

I was determined to make Maubeuge, on the Belgian frontier, before dawn. It was an important communications centre and I thought the Huns might bomb it at dawn – a favourite time. Owens was tiring – he nearly hit several unlighted vehicles – so I gave him my automatic and took over the wheel. Maubeuge was a hell of a long way off, and we had to map-read, which wasn't too easy in the dark. Occasionally we nearly hit unlighted military barriers, and had short sharp arguments with the guards, who insisted that we should douse our lights. A man in a car made a point of stopping us and asking the way to some village I'd never heard of.

'*Anglais?*' he asked, looking suspiciously at my tin hat.

I said I was.

'*Et sans accent?*'

'No, I have an accent.'

He stared into my face, then edged away, and I thought he was pretty rum too. We had no time for argument, so I called 'Good night' and drove on. Everyone was suspect these days, and there was no check. Fifth-columnists and paratroops in all sorts of drag were reported to be abroad, including a bunch of them disguised as nuns! I didn't like it at all.

Soon we came to a *route balisée* – a road with small yellow lanterns along both sides so designed as to be invisible from the air. Long convoys of trucks were streaming up it towards Belgium, without lights and travelling fast. The French had magnificent transport – far superior to our own. Two French guards ordered us to extinguish our lights, quite rightly, shouting: '*Les phares, bon sang! Ils ont bombardé la route toute la nuit!*'

At last we reached Maubeuge. It was four-thirty and already light. I dug the *Commissaire Militaire* out of bed with difficulty. Yes, he had met the young Canadian – he had even had dinner with him, but some French Air Force pilots had taken him to the hotel. Whereupon the *Commissaire* retired hastily back to bed.

I found the hotel. '*Non, pas de pilote anglais.* Never heard of one.' I tried another hotel with the same result. I returned to the unfortunate *Commissaire*, who was positive that Lewis was in the hotel somewhere. Back at the hotel once more I dragged the manager out of bed. '*Non – absolument pas de pilote anglais!*' I went through the same motions at the only other hotel. Mounting frustration made me bloody-minded and I determined to search both hotels from top to bottom. I did, and found Lewis snoring comfortably in bed. I have no doubt that I was one of the most irritating customers to pass through Maubeuge, but the lethargy of those characters was incredible.

We drove to the local airfield to collect Lew's flying kit. The French had a standing patrol of Moranes over the aerodrome, which was an indication of how ineffectual their reporting system was. Then we rattled back to Berry. I caught myself dropping off at the wheel half-way there and handed over to Owens. We kept our tin hats on because German aircraft had been machine-gunning transport on the road, and we couldn't hear much above the engine noise. We left Maubeuge at six-thirty and got back to Pontavert at lunch time.

There was still no news of Billy. I went to his room after lunch to get something and saw his meagre personal possessions spread about, as I had seen those of many another pilot in similar circumstances – a photograph of his mother, a bottle of hair oil, the pyjamas he would need no more. Poor old Billy!

Shortly afterwards I was called to the telephone to speak to Squadron Leader Pemberton at Wing. He said 'There's a message from Rethel hospital to say they have an English officer-pilot there. We think it might be Billy Drake. Will you go out and check?' I was dog-tired, all the benefit of the previous day's rest having been undone, but I got the Bull's permission and tore off again.

The roads were now groaning under refugee traffic, mostly cars from Belgium, Luxembourg and the Sedan district, but the trusty Owens made good speed and we arrived at Rethel at four PM. There was a lot of droning in the sky, and the inhabitants were taking cover. We crossed the railway and bowled up a steep hill to the hospital. Ack-ack guns were firing not far away, and bombs were dropping somewhere else. I left Owens in the courtyard, telling him to take cover, and sprinted across to the hospital wing where 'le pilote anglais' was laid up.

I found him in a room with a French officer – and by God, it *was* Billy! He was lying painfully on his stomach, having been operated on that morning. He told me he had left the flight because he'd run out of oxygen. On the way back to the airfield he saw four Dorniers and attacked them without realizing they had an escort. He got one Dornier, maybe two, but a moment afterwards he was shot up to glory by 110s from behind. He got two bullets in the leg, one in the back, and cannon-shell splinters in the back too. His aircraft caught fire and he baled out. He passed out on the way down, but came to quickly to see tracers whistling past him from the 110s. But as he heard a hell of a battle going on overhead, it's possible that was where the bullets came from. He felt pretty lousy and spoke with difficulty.

As we talked there was the father of bangs outside the window, and the French nursing orderlies started hopping about and ducking behind screens. 'What the hell's that?' I said uneasily. 'Oh, don't take any notice – it's been going on all day,' Billy answered. While bang after bang shook the ward, we went on talking as calmly as possible. We felt we should set some sort of example. The Frenchman in the next bed, a pilot, was badly burnt and knocked about after a nasty smack-up. He was almost in tears, poor bastard. I took a list of things Billy wanted; which included the pyjamas he *did* need after all. Then I left him and went out into the glorious fresh air.

What perfect weather it was. I found the banging was caused, not by bombs as I had thought, but by an ack-ack gun right beside the hospital. Just the place for it! All the townspeople were sheltering in caves in the hillside, some standing at the entrances mutely gazing up at the shoals of German bombers going over westwards. They yelled to me to take cover, but I wasn't going to risk having my transport bombed and being stuck. I found Owens waiting in a doorway. We jumped into the van and shot through the town and over the level crossing beside the station. Bombs were falling near and people were running for shelter. Refugees were lined up beside the road, and as we passed they waved to us to stop and pointed up. I said 'Put your foot down, Owens, we're giving that railway line a bit of a margin' and we belted up the straight tree-lined road.

A quarter of a mile out we pulled up abruptly under a tree hard into the side. We jumped out and I told Owens to throw himself down the banking, shouting to all the refugees in earshot to do the same. The poor bewildered creatures were just standing along the roadside gaping at the sky, whence came the dull roar of multiple engines. I forced a lot of them down the banking and was encouraged to see others further along the road following suit. I then ran down myself with a baby. When the bombs started falling I had to shout at the refugees to make them stay down; they seemed stunned and unable to realize what was happening.

I watched twenty-five Heinkels pass straight overhead at about 15,000 feet and return in sections-echelon-starboard a few minutes later. As we lay flat, stick after stick of high-explosive bombs came whistling down, bursting with crackling roars across the station, the railway, the road and in the surrounding fields.

As the drone of the engines died away I signalled all-clear to the refugees and ran up to the road with Owens. The station was in flames. A heavy pall of dust hung in the air, drifting slowly away in the slight breeze. In the eerie silence the refugees trickled back to their pitiful conveyances. I hoped Billy was OK – the town was still standing. It was beautiful bombing . . . 'Come on, Owens, get cracking!' I said. 'Much more of this and we won't make it!'

We stopped and listened before driving into each town on the way back. We passed Reims-Champagne aerodrome; there was a rash of new holes in it. At last – Pontavert. Poor little Pontavert will be flattened soon, I thought.

Donald Hills dealt with Billy's list, but never took the things to Rethel because the hospital was evacuated next day. The town was later blasted off the map.

I heard quite a bit of news at supper – which consisted of a magnificent salmon caught and presented to the Squadron by Monsignor Paddy Beauchamp, the RAFs senior RC chaplain. Madame Jean had cooked it with her usual genius and given it to Donald and 'Knackers' Henniker, Rolls-Royce's representative with the Squadron, when they called at Bar-le-Duc the previous day to pay our bills. On the way they had passed through Châlons, which is in ruins. Revigny had caught it badly too, but Vassincourt airfield and Bar-le-Duc were still unscathed. There was some talk of our going back to Vassincourt, which curiously was never bombed. The airfield at Berry had been bombed again that evening: the Huns aimed at the fringe of the wood where the Battles had been dispersed.

'B' Flight had tackled a big escorted bomber formation: Boy had shot down a Heinkel and a 110; Prosser, Laurie and Goodman (a new pilot) a Heinkel between them; Laurie had crash-landed with a bullet in the engine and leapt out just before his Hurricane burnt on the ground. Leslie had knocked down a 110 and attacked two Heinkels, shooting one down and landing beside it. The pilot was making a run for it, but the intrepid Leslie chased him on the ground and brought him down with a low flying tackle, later handing him over to the French – but not before he had helped himself to the German's Mauser automatic.

When Sammy was returning from Mézières, after witnessing the sad fate of my beloved aeroplane, he saw a magnificent fight between six Hurricanes and a dozen 110s near Rethel. They were down to 1,000 feet at the end, and Sammy had to double up in a ditch to avoid the machine-gun bullets and cannon shells that were pinging and banging all over the place. He said he would have given his eye-teeth to have a movie camera, and the shots he could have got would have made *Hell's Angels* look really silly. We miss half the fun in the air . . . Sammy watched several 110s come flaming down, and a couple of Hurricanes too. The last Hurricane to leave the scene had evidently run out of ammunition, as it dodged in and out of the trees with a 110 on its tail before eventually shaking it off. The remainder of the 110s pushed off, and Sammy raced across to where one of the Hurricane pilots was dangling from a tree in his parachute-harness. He was alive but in a nasty mess – badly burnt and covered in blood – and scarcely recognizable as Fanny Orton of 73 Squadron. The other pilot to crash was killed. Fanny brought down a couple of 110s in this fight before being knocked down himself; his score was now eighteen German aircraft destroyed.

'A' Flight had also been busy, having met a bunch of Ju 87 dive-bombers – the answer to the fighter pilot's prayer, but the only ones we ever saw. They were escorted by 109s. Hilly took care of a 109 and a Ju 87, Stratton a Ju 87, Sergeant Clowes a Ju 87, and Pussy and Soper a 109 each. Again no one was lost. It seemed miraculous – and it was.

But our nerves were getting somewhat frayed and we were jumpy and morose. Few of the boys smiled now – we were no longer the merry band of days gone by. However, we still had a laugh occasionally, as when we heard the nine o'clock news report by Charles Gardner, BBC observer at Reims, during a bombing raid; we distinctly heard him jump and utter an unscripted 'Ooh!' when a bomb went off in the middle of his broadcast. Or when we heard Leslie's tale of his epic chase after the Hun on the ground, also on the news; we hadn't the energy to chuck Leslie out of the mess, but he was strongly advised to leave voluntarily before we had his trousers off.

Via the news we also heard that the Luftwaffe had been ordered by Hitler to 'harass' refugees: we dearly hoped we'd catch some of them at it. We never did, but that same night we saw evidence that the order was being executed. Sammy, Boy and I met a stream of refugees wending their way through our village. We piled the old Lagonda with food collected from the cookhouse, the mess and storeroom – bread, bullybeef, jam, etc – and distributed two carloads to these unfortunate people.

They surged around us, telling their tragic stories. *This* child's father had been killed by a strafing Hun; *that* young woman's small daughter had had her brains ripped out by a bomb splinter, and so on and on. It was heart-breaking to see these pathetic people, hungry, tired, with fear in their eyes, fleeing before the relentless invader. They were becoming a definite menace to our own forces by blocking communications, and were being deliberately and ruthlessly used by the Germans to heighten the confusion.

We had started out open-mindedly making full allowance for alleged German atrocities; in fact we had complained more that the Germans had made war than at their methods of waging it. But as time went on and they gradually gained the upper hand, as reprisals became less likely, the enemy became more and more ruthless and cruel. His argument may have been that by killing a few thousand refugees he would shorten the war and ultimately save lives; but could any human being worthy of the name deliberately machine-gun helpless old men, women and children?

There was a stony silence in the mess when we told our story. Then a disillusioned Johnny almost reluctantly said, 'They *are* shits – after all.' From this moment our concept of a chivalrous foe was dead. We suddenly saw the war in a grimmer, uglier and no doubt truer light – and we realized we were not just fighting the Germans, but Nazis.

XI

'IL EST FORT, CE BOCHE!'

The morning of 15 May dawned clear yet again; the Germans had certainly made no mistake in their meteorological department. We had been expecting parachute troops at dawn, so were up and about at two forty-five AM. It was 'B' Flight's early turn on the airfield, and shortly after dawn some heavy bombs were dropped on it. Poor old 'B' Flight always seemed to get under the bombs! We relieved them at eight so that they could have breakfast and shake the dirt out of their ears.

Enemy air activity was in full swing again and the sound of bombing was almost continuous, but there was nothing to do about it except hang around, or now and then check the sights on a new aircraft that had been harmonized, i.e. that had had its sights and guns realigned by the armourers. There was a good deal of this to do because none of the aircraft flown over from England to replace our losses had been harmonized before leaving, and some had not been fitted with sights at all. In fact, things came to such a pass that for a precious half day we had only three aircraft serviceable and were forced to inform Wing we couldn't cope with anything sizeable until we got the aircraft sorted out.

About eleven-thirty, six Hurricanes from 'A' Flight were sent off to patrol Reims at 10,000 feet. We hadn't been there more than ten minutes when we heard Pemberton on the R/T from Wing saying 'Much air activity near Vouziers – very many bandits [enemy aircraft] near Vouziers!' We closed in and swung away northeast.

Five minutes later Johnny exclaimed, 'Christ! Close in – close in!'

and we saw them. There were about forty Dorniers in close formation at 10,000 feet, and above them squadron after squadron of 110s stepped right up to 18,000 feet. I counted eighty and gave it up, for everywhere I looked I saw another squadron of them. There must have been well over a hundred and fifty Huns in all. The whole lot were coming straight at us.

Johnny led us to the left, climbing as hard as we could. As we skirted round their right flank Johnny turned towards one of the 110 squadrons at 16,000 feet, saying, 'Here we go – and keep a bloody good look-out!' Fortunately I was doing so and saw another 110 squadron 2,000 feet higher behind us as we were going in. I called over the R/T to indicate them. Johnny answered 'OK Red 3! OK!' and we swerved away and climbed up again flat out.

The top 110 squadron saw us as we reached their level astern of them – they may have seen us before, but they seldom broke formation until attacked. They immediately formed a defensive circle, flying round and round one behind the other. I lost sight of the other Hurricanes and climbed above the circle, then selected a 110 and dived on him from above, finishing in a quarter-attack. Heavy fire came from the Huns' rear guns all round the circle, but I wasn't hit and held fire until I could give my target a long burst close in. Pieces flew off him and flames leapt from his engines. I had time to see him go into a vertical dive as I pulled up violently to avoid being caught by his chum behind, but the air now seemed to be full of Huns and I had to switch my attention to them.

Another 110 squadron had joined in. I don't know whether the circle broke, but looking back on it I think the squadron attacked formed the defensive circle to divert our attention while another squadron attacked us. Anyway, I saw a Hurricane below me being attacked by a 110 and dived on the Hun's tail. He pulled up at about sixty degrees with me still behind him and squirting long bursts savagely into him. Smoke suddenly poured from his aircraft and he fell away to the left with little flames shooting down his fuselage. Just at that moment I heard 'Pop-pop-bang!' and swerved right to see another 110 coming straight up behind me firing for all he was worth. I saw a large cannon-shell hole in my port wing and several bullet holes. A thin trail of whitish smoke was streaming out from underneath my nose, and I said to myself 'This is where I leave!'

I half-rolled violently to the left, went straight under the attacking 110's nose and dived vertically for the ground at full throttle and maximum revs, aileron-turning on the way down. What my speed was at the bottom of the dive I don't know, but it must have been bloody fast – I came down vertically from 18,000 feet. I had a tricky time pulling out, but did so in a gentle spiral, using my tail-wheel carefully and glancing behind. I went right down to ground level before levelling off completely.

Smoke was still spuming from my nose, and I guessed an incendiary had hit the glycol tank and set fire to it. There was no one behind, thank God, so I pulled up to 1,500 feet, throttled back to 170 mph, reduced revs to the minimum and set a south-westerly course. No maps again, but I remembered we'd flown north-east to Vouziers from Reims. The smoke didn't seem to be increasing, though it still poured steadily out. I was flying a new aeroplane with a Rotol constant-speed prop, and I hoped to get it back more or less in one piece providing the fire didn't spread and catch the petrol. I didn't want to crash-land because I thought the thing might go up in flames too low to jump, or explode on the ground, so I opened the hood, unclipped my oxygen tube, and had everything ready to bale out, with the aircraft trimmed slightly nose-down so that the tail would go up as I went out and I wouldn't hit it. I meant to do it in style this time.

In fact I did it in damned bad style. The smoke suddenly increased and turned grey, then enveloped the nose and cockpit. I let go the stick to dive over the side, and naturally as I did so the tail went up (it being trimmed so to do) and I was shot straight up in the air and over it. I was so surprised to find myself in a state of suspension in space that I nearly forgot to pull the ripcord. As I was low down this might have been serious, but I woke up with a curse and pulled the thing so enthusiastically that I tore off a couple of fingernails.

I saw my Hurricane go down in a long curving stream of grey smoke and explode with a dull 'Boom!' in a field. I just had time to roll the ripcord up and put it in my pocket, hoping I wasn't going to land on a barbed-wire fence I could see below, when I was almost on the ground and swinging violently. I hit it with one hell of a thump on a down-swing, doing a couple of somersaults and being nearly knocked out. There was a lot of droning overhead. I didn't want to be ground-strafed, so jumped up and gathered up my parachute, hiding it under a tree.

I looked about me. A couple of fields away was a French peasant with a rifle running towards me. To the other side, across the barbed-wire fence, was a kind of swamp with a small stream running down the middle of it. On the other side of that was a road with a Royal Air Force car racing along it. As the car drew level I waved and it stopped with a screech. A tender following behind also stopped, and a posse of airmen, armed to the teeth, leapt out and advanced in nice open order to the far edge of the swamp. I shouted 'It's OK. I'm British!' Officers tumbled out of the car and called 'Come on over!' Just then the Frenchman behind took a pot at me, but I wasn't particularly interested in him and waved as I climbed the fence with my parachute. I got soaked wading through the swamp, but it was a warm day – and besides, I felt quite pleased with life.

Lord Bill Waleran was in charge of the RAF posse. He was intelligence officer of 75 Wing. As we all shook hands – I proffered my left out of respect for my lost fingernails – there was a roar from an airfield about half a mile away and a column of smoke and dust rose high in the air. 'There goes one of our bombed-up Battles,' said Bill. The Germans were bombing St Hilaire-le-Grand airfield. They shepherded me along to 75 Wing Headquarters in the village of Auberive, where I was given a good and welcome lunch.

The few officers present seemed to think I was taking things very calmly, but I really saw nothing to be disturbed about. I had got over my first experience of baling out; this second effort had been perfectly straightforward, with plenty of time for preparation, and I had rather enjoyed it.

Immediately I arrived at the mess I rang up Air Headquarters at Reims to report that I was all right and asked them to let my squadron know. I spoke to Vincent Stoneham, a friend of mine. When he asked 'Did you get any Huns?' I replied 'No, I don't think so.' The fact was that I couldn't remember a single detail of the fight until two hours later. This is by no means an unusual occurrence and is a strong argument against putting in immediate combat reports, though one not likely to be implemented because of the speed of modern warfare.

After lunch my hosts laid on a car to take me to nearby Reims, where my own transport would be waiting at the *Hôtel du Lion d'Or*. I arrived and took the two drivers in for a drink. I met some of 73's pilots, including Ginger Paul and Cobber Kain. We had a few *coupes* of champagne and swapped news. Cobber told me he had sighted a lone Dornier that morning, but before he had even got within range the whole crew had suddenly baled out!

XII
'NUMBER ONE SQUADRON, SIR!'

got back to Pontavert and found some of the boys having tea in the mess. 'Shot down again, bugger it!' I grunted. They laughed and questioned me about the fight. Apparently we had knocked down a few, Johnny having got a 110, Killy a second, Soper a third, and Clowes a fourth. I claimed one destroyed and one probable, and as they found six lying about the countryside in varying stages of disintegration my probable must have come down. Johnny had been shot in the engine again by a rear gun – that of a 110 he chased to ground-level; as both aircraft were going straight for a belt of high trees when Johnny's engine cut, things were a bit dicey for a moment, but he cleared the trees by inches and put his machine down in a field with the wheels up. He had just come back in a French motor-cycle combination looking highly irritated.

The Bull dished me out a raspberry – quite rightly – for trying to fly a burning aeroplane back. 'I don't care a continental damn about losing an aeroplane – we've got plenty more of those,' he said, 'but I *do* care about losing my pilots. Out straight away next time, Paul!'

The telephone rang and news came through that 'B' Flight had taken off, so we piled into the van and rushed over to the airfield. A large formation of 110s had flown across it at 15,000 feet while Laon was being heavily bombed. This bombing must have been successful, for one of the long fast French convoys that roared continuously along the Reims–Laon road towards the front was now stationary.

'B' Flight were not ordered off, but a little 'B' Flight fitter sprinted up to Prosser and said: 'Come on Sir! Up and at 'em! Come on, Sir!'

Prosser shook his head. 'It's no use now, we'd never catch them at that height.' But the fitter stuck to his guns. 'Oh, come on. Sir! Number One Squadron can't let the cheeky sods get away with that! Come on, Sir! I'll start all the bleedin' kites by meself if you'll go! Number One Squadron, Sir!'

Prosser looked at Boy, Leslie and Laurie; they nodded, and they all raced off to their Hurricanes – much to the little fitter's joy. Just before they took off a formation of Heinkels bombed the airfield. The troops, who had behaved magnificently all along, never flinched, and continued strapping the pilots in and starting up the machines as the bombs came whistling down. The Flight took off through a hail of bombs that burst all over the airfield. They were still up, so they must have engaged.

Boy came back alone, identified by the 'T' on his aircraft. He circled carefully, looking for a clear run through the bomb craters, then landed and taxied in. We got to him as he was climbing out. While we examined the fresh bullet-holes in his machine he told us that they had caught the 110s – thirty of them – because they had turned to come back. Boy shot down two of them and ran out of ammunition. Some of the 110s stuck to him and he really had to work to get away. He finally had to resort to a lot of fancy twisting and turning through trees and other obstructions to shake them off. 'What state my poor flogged bloody engine's in I just don't know!' he said, 'I've never been so scared in my bloody life! Jesus!'

Prosser, Leslie and Laurie were missing: Wing knew nothing, but we felt sure they would show up in due course. Soon Wing had mercy on us and suggested we should relax in the mess, which we did gratefully.

We hadn't been there long when a message came through to say Prosser had baled out, was safe and was on his way back to us. He arrived soon after, alternately cursing and laughing because his trousers were soaked in foul sticky glycol, which never dries out. His eyes were badly inflamed from the stuff. We ragged him a bit and demanded the details.

'Well, it was bloody silly! I only took off because of that crazy fitter – I knew we'd never catch the buggers. But they turned and we got above them. I dived vertically on the leader and fired a burst, allowing deflection, and he just blew up! Nothing left of him but a few chips! Then I pulled up in a climbing turn left and saw a Hun coming at right angles towards me from the left and firing. He wasn't allowing enough deflection and all his shots were wide. I was just turning over him and laughing like hell when my aeroplane was hit by some other bastard behind and I was suddenly drenched in hot glycol. I didn't have my goggles down and the bloody stuff completely blinded me. It hurt like hell! I didn't know where the blazes I was and somehow I went into a spin. I could see sweet fanny and the cockpit was red hot, so I undid the straps and opened the hood to jump out. I couldn't. Every time I tried I was pressed back! I started screaming blue murder, then somehow or other I forced my way out. I came down OK. That's it – now give me a bloody drink!'

Sinking our beers, we mulled over the general situation. There were reports that the Germans had broken through at Sedan; others suggested they had been allowed through for strategic reasons. The Bull told us there was talk of a strategic withdrawal: we might be moving soon. Wing had been bombed in its secret hide-out. We thought the Germans must know we were in Pontavert, and we had again been warned of a paratroop attack. The Bull organized a special guard on the airfield to watch the aeroplanes, and again decreed that we were to sleep in the mess armed. We thought it was rather silly at the time, but he was quite right.

Sammy, Killy and I held a tactics conference. Killy was worried. 'It's odd we haven't had news of Leslie and Laurie yet – the fight was only a few miles away, and they must have come down somewhere near.'

'It won't surprise me if Leslie's bought it,' I said. 'He's been rushing about the sky like a madman for the last five days. He's much too keen to rush into these bloody Huns.'

'I've been thinking the same about you!' said Killy, grinning.

'Yes, you don't want to overplay it,' said Sammy. 'Look at the blokes who knocked up big scores last time – Bishop, Mannock, Richthofen; they only got away with it because they chose the moment to fight and the moment to withdraw. They often refused combat.'

'Always attack! Always attack!' I said, 'regardless of the odds or the position!' I laughed. 'That's what I thought until a couple of days ago. Now I know better!'

We all agreed that, although we were exhausted, the Huns wouldn't be able to keep up the pace much longer either. They were getting things too much their own way, though, and appeared to have anticipated more opposition. They were now coming over in slovenly formations, often without escort. We wondered what the French fighter squadrons were up to. They had shot down seventy-five enemy aircraft on the first day of the *Blitzkrieg*, but we hadn't seen any of them in the air since 10 May. The sky is a big place, but we'd seen plenty of Huns in it.*

Meanwhile the *Luftwaffe* was systematically, and practically without opposition, destroying airfield after airfield, railway junction after railway junction, town after town – and, significantly, no road bridges. Obviously the Germans were blasting a path for their army. This rumoured 'strategic withdrawal' looked pretty rum to us.

As we were about to go into supper a couple of staff cars pulled up and out jumped some brass hats from AHQ at Reims. The Inspector-General of the RAF (the ex-Air Officer Commanding Bomber Command, Ludlow-Hewitt) was with them. We gathered round on the verandah and were solemnly introduced one by one. We looked a rough scruffy gang beside their spit and polish, our overalls filthy, our hair matted, most of us sporting five-day beards – but I think they sympathized. We didn't care much one way or the other.

One of the party, Wing Commander 'Bill' Williams,† asked me 'How are you doing?' I replied, 'Well, Sir, so far we've been lucky and have shot down a few Huns, but I'm afraid we haven't been much use to our bombers. In the first place we never see them because we're always much higher and have to keep our eyes open for the Huns up above, and nine times out of ten we meet enemy fighters before we get to the cover point.'

'And another thing, Sir', I prattled on, determined to ram my points home while I had the chance, 'is that we're operating in penny packets and are always hopelessly inferior in number to the formations we meet. I don't think we should operate in formations of less than two-squadron strength on a bomber cover.'

Bill Williams seemed genuinely interested in my views. We talked

*We now know that most of the French fighter force was engaged in tactical support of the French Army.

†Later Air Marshal Sir Thomas Williams.

a bit more and I was highly embarrassed when he addressed the air marshal, pointing to me, 'Out by parachute twice in three days, Sir!'

'*Four* days actually,' was all I could foolishly mumble.

They didn't stay long and we were left to swallow our supper in peace. We couldn't eat much. The majority of us seemed to have completeley lost our appetites. I forced myself to try because I had noticed the effect hunger had on my morale, but it was always an effort.

After supper a French Army colonel came into the garden. No one took much notice of him and he was naturally irritated. I went across to him and asked what he wanted. His car had broken down in the village – could we mend it? He was most hostile when I asked for his identity card, which he produced under protest. I got a fitter to look at the car: the starter was jammed. His wife was in the car with a stack of luggage. He announced that he was taking her to Paris. They declined my offer of tea or a drink in the mess, but melted a little. The fitter worked on as we chatted by the roadside.

A French *poilu* came cantering up, saluted the colonel and asked: 'Do you know where the such-and-such infantry regiment has gone, Sir? I was asleep in my billet and they left me behind at so-and-so.' I didn't catch the names. The colonel said he didn't know positively, but thought they might have pulled out to a certain place. I tried to catch his eye as more questions were asked, and when the man had gone respectfully suggested it would have been advisable to investigate his identity before answering such questions. The colonel was gruffly disinterested and waved his hand to dismiss the subject. The car was nearly ready. I wondered how a French colonel could take leave at such a moment, but at the same time I was glad he was getting his timid little wife out of it.

The ever-present sound of distant bombing came suddenly nearer, accompanied by the long, melancholy sighing of bombs. It wasn't the ear-splitting, terrifying shriek that whistlers make when falling on you, but a kind of low, menacing moan, an evil echo in the sky. Reims again! A solid formation of Hun bombers came droning over the village on their return trip. I wondered if they would at last flatten little Pontavert. There was a scattering of small cumulus clouds and we stood peering up between them into the clear evening sky.

Then I saw them – maybe fifty Heinkels at somewhere near 18,000 feet, the sinking sun glinting on the pale-blue undersurfaces. A French fighter, a Curtiss, was attacking them singlehanded, but he wasn't pressing his attacks home; perhaps cross-fire was fouling him up. The colonel got very excited and wanted to see one shot down. We were both disappointed that nothing happened. He said sharply: 'Don't you get after these bombers?' and I answered, 'No Sir, that's the French fighters' job, though we've done both jobs up to now.' He glared, then bade me a curt farewell. As I watched their red Citroen disappear in the white dust down the road to Paris I wondered when *we* would see Paris again . . .

When the *Blitzkrieg* had blown off on 10 May, several of our pilots were on leave – Sergeants Berry, Albonico and Clowes – and Leak Crusoe was on an air-firing course. Leave in those days was not supposed to be subject to recall, but they'd been recalled all right, and the three sergeants had just arrived. Their train had stopped fifteen miles the wrong side of Reims and had been bombed several times but not hit. They were astonished at all they saw and heard, and made us five-day veterans feel like seasoned warriors. Leak had been on the train with them, but had last been seen disappearing down the railway track towards Reims on foot.

Just before sunset we were all slouching about in the garden with our indispensable tankards of beer, trying to pick out the Hun formations, as we could hear bombing over towards Reims. We really needed sleep more than anything, but the confounded paratroops were expected to drop in at dusk or dawn, and we naturally wanted to be ready to receive them in the appropriate manner. Visibility was perfect apart from a few fluffy white clouds. Suddenly Boy pointed, and far, far away to the east we could just distinguish a formation of aircraft. We hoisted a cheer as we saw one belch black smoke and start to go down. It went into a spin, still trailing black smoke, at about 20,000 feet. As it was silhouetted against a towering cumulus cloud, I said: 'It looks uncommonly like a Hurricane to me . . .I'm *sure* it's a Hurricane!' The others agreed. 'One of 73 I expect,' said Hilly. We watched, hypnotized, as the spinning aircraft crawled slowly down the cloud mountain, flicking round and round like a dead leaf floating from a tall tree. We tensed as we waited for the white blob of a parachute to appear, for the aircraft to come out of its spin, for it to fall in flames, for the spell to break.

But nothing happened. It just went on spinning. And as it dropped and dropped to the base of the cloud, so did our hopes fall; until finally it disappeared in the evening shadow, leaving only its signature – a crooked trail of smoke down the sky – to mark its last fight.

'Well!' said the Bull abruptly, 'I think that deserves a quick drink!' and we snapped out of it and had one.

XIII
STRATEGIC WITHDRAWAL

At last the red balloon of the sun sank below the trees, the stars came out and the light faded, and we fell on to our camp beds and passed out. The Bull stayed up – I had last seen him bending over the telephone to Wing in a corner of the hall.

It seemed our heads had scarcely hit the straw pillows when we were roused again. It was midnight. There was no longer the struggle back to consciousness as in former days; now we were wide awake in a flash; or, more accurately, we were on our feet, automatically buttoning up tunics and buckling on revolvers, before we realized where we were. We never really slept now. We'd forgotten what sleep was like, forgotten almost the need of it until we found ourselves dropping off over an unwanted meal or during a disinterested conversation.

So we were at it again – moving to Vraux immediately. We didn't know at the time that the Germans were already at Rethel, but in the absence of any instructions from AHQ Reims the Bull had ordered the move on his own initiative.

The air party had to proceed straightaway to the airfield and take the aircraft off an hour and a half before dawn if necessary; if not they would take off half an hour before dawn. Any temporarily unflyable aircraft were to be turned over in bomb craters and burnt. The advance road party, comprising Knackers' Renault, the buckboard, the Renault van, the Bull's Humber brake and a Commer van from Wing with Squadron Leader Pemberton aboard, was to leave now and proceed independently. The main road party, consisting of the remaining Squadron transport, together with the troops, kit, equipment and petrol tankers, was to leave as soon as it was ready.

The Bull's decision was justified by events: the last lorry of the main road party had barely crossed the bridge over the Marne-Aisne canal at Berry at seven AM when it was blown up by French sappers. And Moses, who had returned to try and salvage our mess equipment, was astonished to see French machine-gunners crouching behind cover on the banks of the canal. He was even more astonished when bullets whined overhead and he saw the advance guard of a German *Panzer* unit thundering up the canal. Fortunately the Huns continued along the canal instead of following Moses and the main road party, who were by now haring down the road to Reims.

I was detailed to set off immediately in the buckboard. The idea was to disperse the Squadron so that we should not all suffer the same fate, whatever it might be. As soon as I hauled my kit aboard off we shot – or rather, that was the general idea. But in the darkness we could only crawl against the dense tide of refugees oozing through the village. From time to time we passed a couple of entangled carts and heard excited bickering voices; but in the main they moved silently, the only sounds being the creaks of swaying, rickety carts, the tired cloppety-clop of horses' hooves, the shuffle of weary feet through the dust. It was like a ghost army re-enacting its last retreat.

As we turned out of the village someone stopped us by flashing a torch. A tin-hatted head popped through the window: it was 12 Squadron's doctor, whom I had last seen when I delivered the injured British dispatch-rider to him.

'We seem destined to meet in the middle of the night,' I said with a grin. 'Ah, it's my old chum Richey! Look old boy, can you tell me if this is the road to so-and-so?' I'd never heard of the place, but as I knew where the other three roads went I said it must be. We wished each other good luck and parted. Even that chance meeting seemed curiously unreal.

We gained the Reims–Laon road and turned down it for Reims. I couldn't see my old friend the crucifix, but I knew it was there, and the knowledge was comforting. I often lost sight of God during this period, but I knew He was there, and that was better than food, drink and sleep to me. The main road was clearer – most of the refugees were travelling west across it – but the cars using it were driving much too fast and without lights. We dodged several blazing wrecks piled up in the middle of the road. No one knew whether anyone was trapped inside, no one stopped to find out, no one cared. They must get away! Get away! Get away from the dreaded *Boche*! Frenchmen screamed at us to put our lights out, but we kept them on. Bombs fell beside the road, but we still kept them on. At last we turned off the main road, and just as the pale light of dawn began to tinge the sky we found the airfield. As the light broadened we saw – comforting sight – the sane, strong, sturdy British lines of 114 Squadron's Blenheims glistening in the morning dew.

The Bull soon arrived, followed by Knackers. The first consideration was food, and in this 114 Squadron was very helpful. They patronized a little café a few miles from the airfield, and invited us to share it. The air party roared in soon after dawn, to our relief. We all went down to the café beside a canal bridge in a pleasant rustic setting, and laid waste a very welcome breakfast. We rather swamped the place, but the bomber boys took it sportingly and were most hospitable. A couple of them said they were very happy to have us at hand, as they had just been badly strafed by low-flying Dorniers and several bombed-up aircraft had caught fire and been blown to smithereens: I had seen the sorry remains on the airfield. During breakfast we had the inevitable accompaniment of enemy aircraft engines and bombing: it was Châlons again – some of our pilots had flown over it that morning and said there was nothing left.

Back at the airfield, 'B' Flight were ordered off. While they were up I had a chat with Simon Maude, now a flight commander in 114, whom I hadn't seen since the summer of 1939 in England. In the morning Simon had been bombing a German column from low-level and got a machine-gun bullet through his trousers; it nicked his shin and he was limping slightly. Later, on another mission, he got a bullet from a 109 through the roof of his Blenheim, which grazed his nose and sliced his cheek. Some people are born lucky.

But on this particular morning, he told me, he had returned from his mission to find a bunch of fighters circling Vraux. Actually they were our chaps just arriving, but he thought they were 109s and trundled off to think it out. He circled and watched them land, then approached cautiously to see the Hurricanes taxi-ing in, so he landed. Still dopey after the crack on the shin, he limped over from his machine and met an aircraftsman wearing squadron leader's stripes.

He thought he must be light-headed, and said 'What the hell are you supposed to be?' He was answered somewhat shortly: 'Squadron Leader Halahan, commanding No 1 Squadron. Who the hell are you?' The Bull always wore a tunic made of airman's cloth, finding it warmer and more durable.

'B' Flight returned intact. We had a good lunch at the café, then flopped on the grass under a huge spreading chestnut tree and slept. Or tried to sleep, I should say. Even the light breeze continually disturbed us. I gave it up and went over to talk to another old friend, John Newberry, whom I had last seen in North Wales in 1938. He had been a cheerful blond giant then, and we'd shared many a tramp in the Welsh hills, refreshing long swims in the sea, grogs at the local pub and friendly fights in the mess, smashing tables, chairs and even damaging walls as we had crashed and threshed round the room. I was about to slap him heartily on the back, but another pilot stopped me with an urgent gesture.

He drew me aside and explained that poor old John had been on a low bombing raid and was attacked by 109s. His aircraft caught fire, and he was so low that all he could do was put the thing down fast, bombs and all. He was very badly burnt and shaken-up doing it, but jumped clear before it went up like a flaming torch. Even so, he had returned to try and pull his gunner out. He failed and sustained more burns. Then he ran like hell and threw himself flat as the bombs exploded. He was shot up on the ground by six 109s using their cannon for twenty minutes, but he escaped and managed to get back somehow.

And there he was, straddling a back-to-front chair and trying not to let his eyes betray the agony of his raw back. I tried gently to cheer him up, but he could hardly speak, so I left him alone. Soon afterwards Simon Maude flew him to the English Hospital in Paris.

Our transport arrived late in the afternoon, and when we got to the village long after sunset we had the fag of unloading camp-beds and hoicking them along to our billets. I was allocated a pleasant house beside a lovely old church, and I shared what looked like a bridal suite with Knackers. We tossed for the canopied bed and Knackers won. It was dark, having just gone eleven, but we could still hear German aircraft. There was a stationary French convoy in the village, which didn't reassure us – we didn't want to be bombed by day *and* by night. The owners of the house were two sweet old girls, and proudly showed us the cellar, into which they insisted we must dart at the first bomb. We were secretly determined that nothing would winkle us out of bed that night, least of all bombs. The old girls offered us a drink in the kitchen, and though we were absolutely flogged, we accepted. The kitchen was warm and cosy, hung with a collection of copper pots and pans that glinted dully in the firelight.

Did we think the *Boches* would be here soon? Possibly. Should they abandon their home? Not yet. Would we protect them? We would try. Had we shot down many German aircraft? Some, but we were going to shoot down plenty more. Were we ever frightened? Yes, often! That one bowled them out, and we seized the pause it afforded to take our leave with thanks and good wishes for the night.

We had been in bed about an hour when we were called by a runner and told the Squadron was moving again immediately. Bloody hell! This is becoming a persecution! We rolled out speechless, pulled on clothes and tramped glumly over to Johnny's billet.

The Bull had met a column of French tanks clanking through the village that night moving away from the front. The leading tank had stopped just long enough for an excited French captain to stick his head out of the turret and shout: 'The *Boches* are already in Reims! They will be here before morning!' The tank column then rattled on at full speed. This was disconcerting news, so the Bull had called up AHQ. They didn't know much about the general position, but said they would ring back at nine PM with definite instructions. Nine PM came, but no call, and when the Bull tried to contact Air Headquarters he found the line had been cut. He waited until midnight for communication to be re-established, but it wasn't, so he ordered the move. He was absolutely determined that, whatever happened and whatever orders he disobeyed, 1 Squadron was not going to be wiped out on the ground.

He ordered the same procedure as before. This time we were to go directly to a place variously called Pleurs or Anglure, fifty miles to the south-west.

I was in the air party, and we tramped along to the airfield to await the approach of dawn. It was cold and damp and desolate, and our stomachs trembled with fatigue and hunger. About three AM the telephone rang. It was Panther (AHQ) and a very irate Panther too! Why was the Squadron moving without orders? Rhubarb, rhubarb! Recall them immediately! Rhubarb, rhubarb, rhubarb!

Well, that was that. Here we were with all our beautiful little aeroplanes but no bloody troops, no bloody equipment, no bloody petrol *and* no bloody CO! Johnny tore his hair. A message was sent to Anglure (where 501 Squadron had arrived on 10 May from England). 'B' Flight was left on the airfield for local defence and 'A' Flight went back to the sack. I had a terrible time getting into my billet – the poor old couple thought I was a German paratrooper – but at long last I collapsed thankfully into Knackers' four-poster. The tank captain who had spread the rumour was shot, but as it turned out the poor devil was more or less telling the truth.

I slept like the dead for three hours and was pulled out of bed, much refreshed, to relieve 'B' Flight. The Bull got a raspberry from AHQ, but we thought he was quite right in the circumstances: he had only anticipated a move that came within twenty-four hours anyway. The date, by the way, was 17 May, the day Friday.

Later that morning 'A' Flight were sent off. I protested to Johnny at not being taken along, but he waved me off with 'Not this time, Paul, there'll be plenty more.' Johnny, Pussy, Killy, Hilly and Soper were the five going. Disappointed, I had to be content to watch them take off and wait impatiently for their return. Once again, as I saw them wheel and circle the airfield and climb up and away, I thought what fine men they were.

After an hour and a quarter we began clock-watching, wondering what had happened: they should have been back by now. At last we saw the slender lines of a Hurricane flying towards us; it came over slowly, gently rocking its wings: they'd had a fight! We strained our eyes anxiously for the tell-tale letter on the side: 'H' – Soper. We watched him land between the bomb craters and raced over.

What a bashing he'd had! As he ran the petrol out of his carburettors we stood around counting the bullet and cannonshell holes all over his machine. We were all laughing and Soper raised two fingers derisively.

'How many?' we asked when he climbed out.

'Got two of the bastards – 110s!' he smiled broadly.

'How did they come down?' I asked.

'Flamers!' he said, rubbing his hands. 'And one of them was the bugger who did this lot!', waving at his scarred machine. The tally was three cannon-shell holes and thirty bullet holes: one bullet had entered the fuselage, passed through the harness slit in the armour plating behind Soper's back and stopped at the harness cable just short of his neck. There were numerous dents in the armour plating; thank God we had the stuff – it had already saved several of our lives. Soper did a fantastic job in bringing his Hurricane back: one of the aileron hinges was severed and all his controls were damaged. We wrote the aircraft off on the spot.

Soon all the Flight but one came trickling back. Johnny, Hilly, and Killy had each shot down a 110. Pussy was missing. He was missing all morning. When this happened we ignored it, didn't even mention the name. It wasn't a conscious effort at tact – we no longer knew the meaning of the word – but an automatic reticence, a reluctance to discuss possibilities of which each one of us was only too well aware.

And Pussy turned up all right, as most of us had. He had shot down a 110, gone down in flames himself and baled out. This was his second bale-out, and the French had taken advantage of the situation by using him for target practice as he floated down. They invariably assumed that anyone in a parachute was automatically a Hun. Pussy was greatly discomforted as some thirty rifle shots whined past him, but when he hit the ground he turned his excellent command of the more colourful side of the French language to good account. His eloquence even surprised the soldiers!

Still no news of Leslie and Laurie. Gradually we began to give up hope. We didn't have much time to think about them, but they were always in the back of our minds. A rumour buzzed round the squadron that Leslie had been seen the previous day going into a café in a certain village, but this was finally discounted.

Laurie, who had been posted to us in France from 87 Squadron, was as good a pilot as any and better than some; but he had been dogged by consistent bad luck since the *Blitzkreig* started – and this made the third time he had been shot down in five days. He already had three Huns to his credit, and had no doubt increased his score in the last fight. Leslie, on the other hand, had been lucky. He was Australian, and had thrown himself into the fray with a reckless abandon that was magnificent and typical of other of his countrymen I had known. He had shot down a total of seventeen enemy aircraft, most of them in five days, without once being clobbered himself. He too would certainly have increased his score before going down. He did not know he had been awarded the Distinguished Flying Cross. We never saw or heard of these two boys again and they are now officially presumed killed in action.

During supper that evening we reviewed the *Luftwaffe's* tactics. It was agreed they didn't like our Hurricanes, few as they were, for as a sequel to Cobber Kain's story of the Dornier crew baling out immediately they saw him, a new pilot, Peter Boot, had sighted a formation of five Dorniers which had split up and beaten it when he appeared alone. On the other hand the Huns were showing no signs of cowardice in combat – though they were usually in such vastly superior numbers that there would have been no excuse for doing so. What we had seen of German bombing had been devastatingly effective, partly due to accuracy and partly to a ruthless disregard of non-military incidentals surrounding the targets. We were appalled by the strafing of refugees, but considered that the individual German airman was carrying out his orders accurately and well, and on the whole fighting like a gentleman.

But we hadn't wanted this bloody awful war that the Huns seemed to think so glorious. We had been forced to fight. 'And now that we *are* fighting,' we thought, 'we'll teach you rotten Huns *how* to fight! We'll shoot your pissy little fighters out of the sky, we'll rip your dirty great bombers to shreds, we'll make you wish to Christ you'd never *heard* of the aeroplane! We'll teach you the facts of war!' And we knew we could – *if we were reinforced*.

We were sure we had the measure of the Germans. Already our victories far exceeded our losses, and the Squadron score for a week's fighting stood at around the hundred mark for a deficit of two pilots missing and one wounded. We knew the Huns couldn't keep going indefinitely at that rate, but we also knew *we* couldn't keep it up much longer without help. We were confident that help would soon come. *We reckoned without Dowding*.

What we could not understand was why we were not being used to intercept the massive enemy bomber formations that were hammering hell out of France. The aircraft we had shot down had been met mainly by chance. We were even forbidden to take off when our own airfield was under attack. We knew that the plan was for us to provide cover for British bombing raids against the German Army, while the *Armée de l'Air* was delegated to deal with enemy raids. But the plan had manifestly broken down: British bombers were being thrown away piecemeal on work left undone by the Allied armies, such as the destruction of bridges; we were trying to cover our bombers against hopeless odds; the French fighters were desperately striving to protect their crumbling armies; and the French high command appeared to us to have become a victim of German sabotage. We were convinced that all available RAF fighters should now do their proper job: the interception and destruction of German bombers. Losses would have been higher, but we knew we could treble our victories. Meanwhile the 'strategic withdrawal' continued. . .

After this solemn analysis Johnny confided to me: 'Keep it under your hat, Paul, but the Squadron is shortly to be re-formed. The twelve of us who've done all the work are to be relieved.'

I was stunned, and countered rather stupidly: 'Why? This is only the beginning!'

'Well, good God!' Johnny snapped. 'You don't think we can keep this insane pace up much longer, do you? Anyway, the Bull has told AHQ that he refuses to continue with his present pilots and they'll be bumped off from fatigue if he does. So there it is.'

Yes, there it was. It was grim news for all of us. It would be a hell of a wrench to leave dear old 1 Squadron, that even the *Luftwaffe* had failed to knock apart. But I tried to comfort myself with the thought that we'd all return to it one day . . .

XIV
THE LAST BATTLE

Our transport and kit left for Anglure later that night. We slept at 114 Squadron's hut on the airfield and took off at six. We had quite a job locating Anglure, which turned out to be an undefined collection of fields, some cultivated and sprouting vegetables of various kinds and some recently harrowed, dotted with clumps of pine trees. It even boasted a big thicket slap in the middle, and but for 501 Squadron's Hurricanes parked on it we'd never have picked it out. At least the natural layout provided excellent camouflage, which was something.

Nothing much happened that morning beyond a few local patrols. But at about three, volunteers were called for to make up a formation of eight to fly to Amiens. A small voice inside me tempted 'Don't be a sap – leave it to some of the fresh chaps – you'll be going home in a day or two if you're smart . . .' I volunteered. Hilly was leading and would take three with him. I would follow with another three. The majority chosen were pilots who'd joined the Squadron shortly before the *Blitzkreig* to enable us to work in shifts, but we hadn't used them up till now because they were completely inexperienced. Our orders were to go to Amiens, land and refuel, and then do the special job to be allotted to us. We were doubtful whether we could make Amiens in one hop, but set off.

The going was smooth until we reached St Quentin. A lot of light flak opened up on us, and as we were flying at 1,000 feet it was pretty hot. We split up at once, turning, diving and climbing individually to scatter the target. The Germans weren't supposed to be within fifty miles, but this stuff was too accurate to be French. It was

The *Luftwaffe* in France in 1940 was built around half a dozen types of fighting aircraft, all of which we ultimately encountered in huge numbers.

The Messerschmitt Me 109E3: one man, 1,100 horsepower, two machine guns and three cannon (though only two were fitted for operations). With a much higher speed, rate of climb and ceiling than our Hurricanes and far better armed, the 109 could not turn as tightly in a dogfight. But the German pilots could often shake us off by 'bunting', or pushing the stick forward to dive. We could not follow this manoeuvre because our carburettors were unable to feed fuel into the cylinders under the resulting negative-g conditions. *Ét Ciné-Armées*.

Messerschmitt Me 110 *Zerstörer* (Destroyer) fighter crews brief for a patrol over the Maginot Line, early spring 1940. Note the neat helmets and goggles, thick overalls and gauntlets, and Luger automatic pistols. Each 110 (background) packed two men, 2,200 horsepower, five machine guns and two cannon. *Bundesarchiv*.

Three Messerschmitt Me 110s of ZG.52 in close formation. With level and diving speeds, climb and armament all better than those of the Hurricane, the 110 could fortunately not out-turn us. *Bundesarchiv*.

A Dornier Do 17Z bomber/reconnaissance aircraft climbs through broken cloud for a recce over France, its 2,000 horsepower hauling three men, four machine guns and three automatic cameras. Comparatively fast and high-flying, the Dornier was Germany's main long-range reconnaissance weapon against France in the winter of 1939–40 and was difficult to overhaul in a tailchase. *Bundesarchiv.*

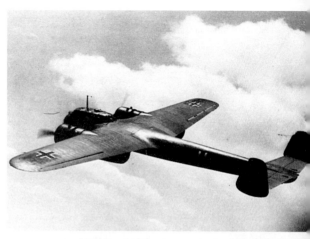

The pilot and bomb aimer/front gunner of a Dornier take it easy before reaching oxygen height (15,000 feet). Note the lightweight helmets with flat ear pads and neatly positioned R/T leads, and back-type parachutes. The lock on the front gun (similar to that with which Frankenberger shot down Pussy Palmer on 23 November 1939) is visible over the gunner's head, and the pilot's ring-and-bead sight can be seen through the port windscreen. *Bundesarchiv.*

A Dornier Do 17Z of III/KG.76, bomb doors open, runs up to its target during the battle to unload 1,000 kilograms of bombs. Comparatively manoeuvrable, the Dornier was used very successfully for individual attacks against small targets, in small formations against airfields and in large ones for high-level pattern bombing. The fields of fire of its machine guns dictated attacks from dead astern (as Boy Mould noted on 30 October 1939, when he shot down the first German aircraft to be destroyed by the RAF in France since 1918). *Bundesarchiv.*

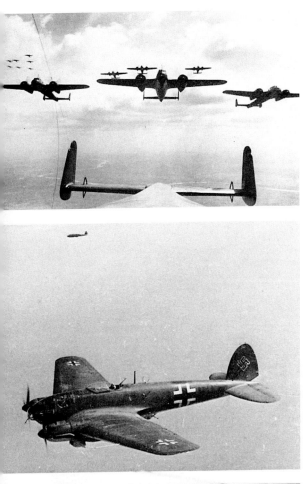

A formation of Dornier Do 17Zs of KG.3 climbs away from its base near Frankfurt-am-Main during the battle and crosses the Rhine at Worms, course set for Nancy. By the time they cross the French frontier they will have closed up into tight formation and probably picked up an escort of Me 110s. It was with an escort of fifteen 110s covering a formation of thirty Dorniers that five of us fought the battle on 11 May and shot down ten of them. *Bundesarchiv.*

A pair of Heinkel He 111P-4s of KG.1 *Hindenburg* split up above thick haze to attack pinpoint targets: five men, 2,200 horsepower, five to six machine guns and 2,200 kilograms of bombs to each aircraft. Biggest and slowest of the *Luftwaffe*'s twin-engined bombers, the Heinkel carried the heaviest defensive armament but was an easy fighter target on its own because of its lack of speed and manoeuvrability and large blind spot dead aft. *Bundesarchiv.*

This Heinkel has been obliged by the haze to descend to low altitude to identify and bomb its target, and the shortage of Allied fighters allows it to get away with it. Carrying the heaviest bomb load of all *Luftwaffe* bombers, the Heinkel provided a steady bombing platform. *Bundesarchiv.*

A formation of Heinkel He 111P-4s heads east towards Germany after dropping its bombs on France. The Heinkel was at its best in large formations because of the weight of bombs it could drop simultaneously and the mutual defensive support each aircraft could give the others. *IWM*.

The observer hangs over the side of a Henschel Hs 126 short-range reconnaissance aircraft during the battle to photograph a convoy as a companion aircraft formates: two men, 850 horsepower, two machine guns and 100 kilograms of bombs, the Hs 126 gave the German Army invaluable up-to-the-minute information in the battle. But it was a dead duck if it met an enemy fighter. *Bundesarchiv*.

Most publicized and most feared of all the *Luftwaffe*'s bombers in 1940 was the Junkers Ju 87B *Sturzkampfflugzeug* ('Stuka') dive-bomber: two men, 1,200 horsepower, three machine guns and 500 kilograms of bombs. Slow and virtually defenceless, the Stuka could only operate under friendly fighter cover or in the total absence of enemy fighters. Attacking pinpoint targets in close co-operation with the German Army, the Stuka was often the only enemy bomber Allied troops ever saw and most of its fearsome reputation stemmed from them. The devastation it caused could not approach that spread by a large formation of high-level bombers, but its ear-drum-splitting intimidating method of attack terrified troops, and it could drop the *Luftwaffe*'s largest bomb on a small target with maximum physical and psychological effect.

A flight of six Stukas heads for Sedan in close formation. *Ét Ciné-Armées.*

The Stukas break up over the objective to select their individual targets. *Bundesarchiv.*

The leading Stuka peels off over the vertical. *Ét Ciné-Armées.*

The moment after release: an automatic device eases the bomber out of its near-vertical dive at the right moment and correct airframe loading for safety. Stukas were responsible for breaking through the French front for the German Army. *Ét Ciné-Armées.*

Latest, fastest and most versatile of the *Luftwaffe*'s bombers in 1940 was the Junkers Ju 88A: four men, 2,400 horsepower, three machine guns and 1,800 kilograms of bombs. Fast, manoeuvrable and difficult to catch, the Ju 88s we saw in our area were used exclusively for reconnaissance or individual low-level attacks, and never in formation. One of them was unlucky enough to run into Killy early in April and they shot each other down.

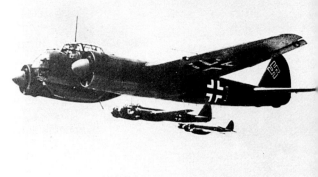

This Ju 88 was shot down by Royal Artillery gunners as it strafed an RAF airfield in France during the battle and is being minutely examined by an RAF technical team. The hole from a 40-millimetre Bofors shell can't have done the crew much good. *IWM.*

y the time the Second World War began, the
oncept of the successful fighter pilot as a supreme
id selfish individualist had long been replaced
the Royal Air Force by that of the team. In no
AF fighter squadron can this concept have been
ore intensely cultivated than in No. 1. But if
Squadron's success in the air fighting in France
in be largely attributed to this, it should also be
membered that the squadron benefited from two
cher exceptional factors working in combination:
.e length of time its pilots had trained together
peacetime, which averaged at least three years,
nd the eight months it had spent skirmishing
ith the *Luftwaffe* over the Franco-German
ontier before the big battle. No. 1's achievements,
nique in the annals of the RAF, should be seen
gainst this background. The Squadron shot down
14 enemy aircraft in ten days for the loss of two
ilots presumed killed in action, two wounded in
ction and one prisoner of war, and was awarded
n Distinguished Flying Crosses and three
istinguished Flying Medals for those ten days of
ghting. Here is the team.

The Bull (left) Squadron Leader P. J. H.
Halahan DFC (Irish), the commanding officer.
He survived the war. *IWM.*

Johnny (right): Flight Lieutenant P. R. Walker
DFC (English), second-in-command and flight
commander of 'A' Flight. He shot down the first
Messerschmitt Me 110 to fall to Allied fighters
in France and was twice shot down facing rear
guns. He survived the war.

'rosser: Flight Lieutenant P. P. Hanks DFC
English), brilliant pilot, flight commander of
3' Flight. He survived the war. *IWM.*

Hilly: Flying Officer M. H. Brown DFC
(Canadian), 'A' Flight, our second top-scorer.
He was killed in action in 1941 leading his
fighter wing on a low-level attack from Malta
on a German airfield in Sicily. *IWM.*

Leslie: Flying Officer L. R. Clisby DFC (Australian), 'B' Flight, No. 1's top scorer. He was presumed killed in action on 15 May. *IWM*.

Killy: Flying Officer J. I. Kilmartin DFC (Irish), 'A' Flight. He shot down the first Ju 88 in Worl War II. He survived the war. *IWM*.

Pussy: Flying Officer Palmer DFC (Anglo-American), 'A' Flight, was shot down three times by front guns. He was killed in action in 1942 leading his fighter squadron over Brest. *IWM*.

Paul: Flying Officer P. H. M. Richey DFC (Irish Australian), 'A' Flight. He shot down the Squadron's first fighter, an Me 109. *IWM*.

Boy: Pilot Officer P. W. Mould DFC (English), 'B' Flight. He shot down the first German aircraft destroyed by the RAF in France since 1918. He was killed in action off Malta in 1941. *IWM*.

Billy: Flying Officer B. Drake (English), 'B' Flight. He survived the war.

Stratters: Pilot Officer Stratton DFC (New Zealander), 'A' Flight. He survived the war. *IWM*.

Clowes: Sergeant-Pilot Clowes DFM (English), 'A' Flight. He survived the war. *IWM*.

Soper: Sergeant-Pilot Soper DFM (English), 'A' Flight. He was killed in action as a squadron leader in England in 1941. *IWM*.

Berry: Sergeant-Pilot Berry DFM (Scottish), 'B' Flight. He shot down the Heinkel that sank the SS *Lancastria* with the loss of 3,000 lives. He was killed in action in 1940 in the Battle of Britain. *IWM*.

Two stars of 73 Squadron: Top Scorers

Fanny (left): Flying Officer N. Orton DFC (English). He was killed in action leading his fighter squadron from England in 1942.

Cobber (right): Flying Officer E. J. Kain DFC (New Zealander), great pilot, media megastar. He was killed on active service in France doing flick-rolls at 100 feet. *IWM*.

Farewell to France. Châteaudun, 14 June, 1940.

Just out of hospital, Paul Richey poses with the fin of one of the two Me 110s he destroyed in battle over Rumigny on 11 May, when five Hurricanes of No 1 Squadron attacked a formation of thirty Dornier 17s and fifteen Messerschmitt 110s, destroying ten 110s for the loss of one Hurricane, all confirmed on the ground by the gendarmerie. Notches on the stick marked personal score of victories.

Some of 'the friends I left behind'

There was one essential difference between the Allied pilot who fought in the RAF and his British peers: his country was occupied by the Germans. In the unique case of France the occupation had been cynically contrived to divide the country morally and physically. It was therefore more difficult for a Frenchman, especially a serving officer, to decide where his first duty lay. Having once decided to quit his country, he had to turn his back on family and friends and deliberately to abandon them to the horror of enemy occupation and to the possibility of German revenge. Hence the *nom de guerre*. The road to London or even Algiers was thus beset not only with constant risk to the escaper, but with the nagging mental torment of anxiety for others. I always felt that every Frenchman who was fighting for his country and for ours with the RAF had fully lived up to its motto, *Per Ardua ad Astra*, while still proudly wearing the flying badge of the *Armée de l'Air* with its equally mystical symbolism: 'The Wings bear me, the Star guides me, the Wreath awaits me'– the wreath of victory, or of the death for others that is victory? The following selection of some of the French pilots I was privileged to know in 1940 is small but typical, while the two ladies included with them are representative of the underlying strength of France – her women.

La Popote des Ailes, Villacoublay, Paris. They were all gay, reckless and courageous – what we in the RAF call "regardless" – as only French pilots can be.' The last lunch at Viroflay, five days before the Germans entered Paris, before a surrender that none of us thought was possible. *La Mémère* – **Madame Henriette Puyade**, *Médaille de L'Aéronautique* - is in the centre. The men (left to right) are **Jean Cliquet**, test pilot for the Morane fighter company, who survived the war: **Jacques Fickinger**, chief test pilot for the Amiot bomber firm and my host, killed on active service in 1943; myself with poodle; *Capitaine* **Pierre Casanova** of Air France, shot up with me by British guns in 1939 and killed flying for his company in 1942; **Daniel Rastel**, chief test pilot for SNCASO Bloch, who escaped the Germans to join the Free French Air Force's Alsace fighter squadron in England and survived the war to test again for Dassault; **Jérôme Cavalli**, chief test pilot for the Gourdou et de Sueur fighter company, who escaped to North Africa to become a brilliant fighter pilot in the Groupe Lafayette of the *Armée de l'Air* and was killed in 1943, while playing pétanque on his airfield, by the last bomb from the last German bomber to attack Algeria; and (last on right) **Lebeau**, chief test pilot for the Lioré et Olivier firm, killed during the battle delivering a Le0 45 bomber/reconnaissance aircraft to the *Armée de l'Air* on 23 June, 1940, two days before the Franco-German ceasefire. **Charles Fatôme**, later engaged in and to survive British-directed secret operations in France, took the picture with my camera, and **Maurice Claisse**, chief test pilot for Breguet, who 'showed me round pointing out various photographs', had to leave before it was taken.

La Mémère ran the *Popote des Ailes* from 1927 to 1955 for the civil and military pilots from the *Centre des Essais en Vol*, the *Ecole d'Application de l'Aéronautique*, *Avions Breguet* and prototype testing teams from France's leading plane-makers. A much-loved mother figure to them all, she shed a mother's bitter tears on the frequent occasions on which she had to remove for ever their places at table. Her *Livre d'Or*, starting in 1930 with the signature of Costes, first man to fly the Atlantic from Paris to New York, contained all the illustrious names in French aviation between the wars, and I was honoured to be asked to sign it at our lunch. Maurice Claisse returned to Paris after the Franco–German armistice to write in it: '*Aujourd'hui, 1er août 1940, tout seul je rouvre la Popote. Vivent les Ailes Françaises!*' But the

Popote closed again shortly afterwards. Four years later to the day a joyful *Mémère* wrote in the Livre d'Or: '*Colonel Maurice Claisse des Forces Françaises Libres retour d'Angleterre*'. 'We were just a few for her last trip,' Maurice wrote to me after *La Mémère's* funeral in 1977, and indeed only a few of 'her' pilots were left. They included Colonel Bernard Dupérier, who wrote next day: 'Round Claisse and Detré the old hands were gathered, white haired and wrinkled by so many flights, so many exploits, so many memories. But also there, still remembered by the survivors as they had been when killed and whose presence was almost palpable, were all those whose places at table had been removed at the *Popote des Ailes*.' *Author.*

Maurice: Lieutenant-Colonel Maurice Claisse, *Armée de l'Air* and Free French Air Force, chief test pilot for *Avions Breguet*, holder of five international helicopter records, and test pilot on twenty-five pre-war prototypes, including the 690 series of low-level bombers. Starting at dawn on 11 June 1940, he and two of his pilots performed the remarkable feat of flying seventeen serviceable aircraft the 250 miles from Paris to Cognac in two and a half days. They included the brand-new Breguet 697 bomber prototype, which Maurice flew out three hours before the German Army took Villacoublay airfield. Three days later he placed the seventeen aircraft, two pilots, one mechanic and himself under the

orders of the newly arrived *54th Escadre d'Attaque*, but at Toulouse the next day all bombing missions were suddenly cancelled and the armistice was announced on the radio. Claisse and Lenoble immediately tried to seize their aircraft but, finding all the propellers removed, instead hijacked Louis Breguet's 40 hp Renault from the Toulouse works and tried to catch the last Allied withdrawal from Biarritz: they got there with the first SS Panzers. After two attempts to reach England from Brittany in fishing vessels, Claisse left Paris with Jacques Fickinger, Jérome Cavalli and two others on 3 January 1941, and later walked across the Pyrenees with Spanish guides in three days and two nights. They reached Gibraltar in April. By August, aged 36, he was commanding a flight in an RAF Spitfire squadron in Cornwall where I found him again in 1942 during a tour of inspection with the commander-in-chief of Fighter Command, Air Marshal Sir Sholto Douglas. I persuaded the C-in-C to post Maurice to the RAF's experimental establishment at Farnborough, but not before he had flown 130 hours on operations and 68 offensive missions over enemy-occupied France. In eighteen months at Farnborough he tested 70 different types of British, American and captured German aircraft and became the first French jet pilot (on the first British jet, the Gloster E.29/38 prototype). Barred at the age of thirty-eight from fighter operations, he volunteered for night fighters and flew a further 130 operational hours over the Allied invasion fronts. A pre-war *Chevalier de la Légion d'Honneur 'à titre exceptionnel'*, he finished his service in the *Armée de l'Air* with the French Croix de Guerre with two palms, and both the British and

American Distinguished Flying Crosses. He was also promoted *Commandeur de la Légion d'Honneur*, made a *Compagnon de la Libération* and awarded the *Médaille de l'Aéronautique*. He returned to testing to complete 4,000 flying hours on 180 different types of aircraft. Here he is at Farnborough in the cockpit of a Spitfire IX specially modified for compressibility trials, which he dived under control at Mach 0.91, faster than the Meteor jet could subsequently achieve. *Maurice Claisse*.

St Ex: Capitaine Count Antoine de Saint-Exupéry, *Armée de l'Air* – a photograph taken before mobilization. '. . . A French Air Force captain . . . performed conjuring and card tricks, choosing me as his subject. He was an exceptionally skilful and amusing fellow . . .' Still celebrated today for his writings, especially about flying, St Ex was for many years a mail and airline pilot in France, North Africa and South America before being mobilized as a reserve captain in the 2nd Escadrille of the *Armée de l'Air's* distinguished 33rd Bomber/Reconnaissance Groupe, our friends and neighbours. He describes his part in the battle, flying the brand new Bloch 174, in his great book *Pilote de Guerre (Flight to Arras)*. Escaping from France to North Africa, he fought the Germans again under General Giraud after the American landings. Completing a second operational tour in 1943, he had just been taken off operations when he characteristically volunteered to replace an absent pilot for an extra night mission and failed to return. There is some evidence to show that his P-38 Lightning fighter was shot down into the sea off Corsica by a JU 88 night fighter operating from France. *Ét Ciné-Armées*.

Fifi: *Capitaine* Jacques Fickinger, *Armée de l'Air*, chief test pilot for *Avions Amiot*, with one of his babies, the Amiot 370 prototype, which in 1938 established a number of international distance records. 'On the way he spoke about the new Amiot heavy bomber he was testing: with Rolls-Royce Merlin engines, he'd got it up to 330 mph at 18,000 feet – very nearly as fast as the Hurricane.' This was the Amiot 356 bomber, a parallel development to the 370 and in practice faster than the Hurricane. Prevented from flying it to England as he intended when the Germans took Paris, on 3 January 1941 Fickinger left Paris with Maurice Claisse, Jerome Cavalli and two others and managed to reach Vichy, where the party split up. Fickinger and Cavalli made their way to Algeria, where they rejoined the *Armée de l'Air* under General Giraud when the Americans landed in 1943. Later that year this great and much-loved pilot was accidently killed while flying a Lockheed Hudson on a supply mission to Corsica. *Alla Dumesnil*.

Moses: Lieutenant-Colonel Demozay (*nom-de-guerre* **Morlaix**, his home town in Brittany), *Armée de l'Air* and Free French Air Force. 'Although he had not flown for five years, had never flown a twin, and had no maps, he got a fitter to start the engines and flew the old crate to England with fifteen jubilant RAF troops aboard.' The exploit of 1 Squadron's French interpreter in leaving France with us became a legend in the RAF. Trained by us as a fighter pilot at the fighter school formed in England by the Bull after the battle, Moses later shot down some twenty German aircraft and commanded an RAF fighter squadron. Here he is in French uniform wearing the *Légion d'Honneur*, the French *Croix de Guerre* with at least a dozen palms, the British Distinguished Service Order, the Distinguished Flying Cross and Bar, and the Czech War Cross. *Ét Ciné-Armées.*

Adal: *Capitaine* Count Adalbert de Segonzac, Free French Air Force. A pre-war private pilot in England and a reserve cavalry officer in the French Army, he galloped into 1 Squadron's officers' mess at Neuville to establish friendly relations on behalf of his regiment and was thereafter my frequent host at his brigade head-quarters at Sermaize. In action in the Ardennes with his mechanized reconnaissance unit early in the battle, he was severely wounded. Early in 1941 he tried to reach England through a British-run intelligence network operating from Lyons, but narrowly escaped arrest by the Gestapo at Nantes. Crossing back into Vichy France, he escaped to Algeria, marched into Morocco, and then continued to Tangier with false identity papers. A Spanish fishing vessel smuggled him to Gibraltar, and by July 1943 he was flying Spitfires in an RAF fighter squadron. After a year of offensive operations over France, he joined the Cigogne squadron of the *Armée de l'Air* for the Allied invasion of Europe. In November 1944 he was shot down over the Rhine, landing in enemy-occupied Holland and became a prisoner of war. He was awarded the *Croix de Guerre* with five palms and the British Distinguished Flying Cross, and was made *Officier de la Légion d'Honneur* and *Officier de l'Ordre du Mérite*. Here he is in London in 1943. *Adalbert de Segonzac.*

Bernard: Lieutenant-Colonel Bernard Dupérier, *Armée de l'Air* and Free French Air Force. His first hundred operational hours in the *Armée de l'Air* were flown ten years before World War II against rebels in Morocco. While serving with the reserve he became a qualified aircraft engineer, designed, built and flew his own amphibian, designed and built air-propellered boats, and tested Dutch Koolhoven aircraft for the French SAFA company. Recalled to the colours in 1939, on 9 September he volunteered for the first and only operation of the war by his unit, the 4th Escadrille of the 32nd Bomber Escadre – a daylight reconnaissance by seven Bloch 200 bombers (maximum speed 130 mph) of Trier in Germany; only two aircraft returned. His Groupe was withdrawn to Morocco during the battle to re-equip with Douglas Bostons and rushed to Tunisia to bomb Italy when the armistice intervened. He escaped to England in April 1941, via Algiers, Casablanca, Lisbon, New York and Montreal, and was posted straight to an RAF anti-shipping Hurricane fighter squadron. He later commanded a flight in the first Free French fighter squadron, the *Ile-de-France*, in Spitfires, then became squadron commander after his CO, Commander (later Admiral) de Scittivaux was shot down over occupied France and his wing leader, the British ace, Wing Commander Michael Robinson, was presumed killed in action with his No. 2, the French Lieutenant Maurice Choron. Bernard took command of the Free French Alsace fighter squadron in 1943. He later commanded the RAF's Biggin Hill Wing and then the Free French fighter wing comprising the *Ile-de-France*, *Alsace* and *Cigogne* squadrons. Posted to French air headquarters in 1944 and then to General Koenig to help prepare the Allied invasion of France, he volunteered on 4 August 1944, at the age of thirty-seven, to parachute into Brittany behind the German lines near St Brieuc which he liberated at the head of the local partisans. Next day he was severely wounded by an anti-tank shell. For that operation, his 160 missions over enemy-occupied France, seven air victories and several aircraft damaged, and numerous successful attacks on German ships, he was awarded the French *Croix de Guerre* with ten palms, both British and American Distinguished Flying Crosses, and the Czech War Cross. He was also made a *Grand Officier de la Légion d'Honneur*, a *Compagnon de la Liberation* and an officer of the Order of the British Empire, and was awarded the *Grand Croix de l'Ordre du Mérite* and the *Grande Medaille d'Or l'Aero Club de France pour Faits de Guerre*. He became Deputy to the *Assemblée Nationale*, president of the *Aero Club de France* and of the *Association Pour le Soutien du General de Gaulle*. Here he is as *Commandant* Dupérier in his Spitfire VB in 1943. *Ét Ciné-Armées.*

Count Alec Castéja of the ler Chasseurs à Cheval. Injured in the fighting in the French Ardennes, he later spent a year in the hands of the Gestapo for his work in the Resistance. *Author.*

Alla: Commandant Alla Dumesnil (*nom de guerre* **Dupont**). Daughter of the French Admiral Dumesnil, who fought in World War I alongside the British in the Dardanelles, she spent her early childhood in London and remained a confirmed Anglophile. Owner of vast plantations in Kenya, Alla abandoned them at the outbreak of World War II to return to Paris to serve her country. On 8 November 1939, a lunch at the legendary *Popote des Ailes* inspired her with the spirit and tradition of the French airman and catapulted her into his world. Escaping to London when France was overrun and ordered by the Vichy-sympathizing French Ambassador either to return to France or have her passport withdrawn, she threw it into the fire in front of him and later took out an alien's card. In London she founded the *Formation Féminine de l'Air* or *'Filles de l'Air'* (the Free French Air Force equivalent of the RAF's Women's Auxiliary Air Force), which reached a strength of 12,000 women and girls of French origin in England. Here she is being decorated by *General de l'Armée Aérienne* Bouscat, chief of staff of the *Armée de l'Air*, with the *Légion d'Honneur* and the *Croix de Guerre* at the Paris airfield of Issy-les-Moulineaux after the war.

And a man of peace: **Professor Count Thierry de Martel.** Perhaps the greatest of them all because he gave his life in saving life. After spending the whole of World War I removing German metal from the heads of French soldiers, between the wars he became world famous as France's foremost neurosurgeon. Throughout the battle in 1940 he operated for twenty-one out of every twenty-four hours for five solid weeks removing more German metal from more French soldiers' heads at the American hospital at Neuilly-sur-Seine, Paris, and saved hundreds of lives, including my own when it was placed by the grace of God in his wonderful hands. He could easily have escaped from the Germans but chose to continue saving lives as long as possible and to stand by his patients until alternative medical attention for them was at hand. Worn out and heartbroken, he took what was left of his own life as the German Army marched into Paris on 14 June 1940. Here he takes a breather on the roof from which his American colleague Doctor Rogers and I watched the bombing of Paris on 3 June. *AFP.*

first-rate shooting: black flak bursts appeared in clumps of four all over the place, at the right height and uncomfortably close; and there was some smaller stuff that formed a ring when it burst, leaving hardly any smoke. Ack-ack bursts always looked like spooks to me, suddenly popping out and pulling frightening faces.

We had broken up and turned to head back when one of the Hurricanes dived and disappeared. I saw three aircraft that I at first took to be 110s. I got into position to attack, but they were Potez 63s dive-bombing. One of them was hit by flak and went down in flames. It was now obvious that the Germans, as usual, weren't where they were supposed to be. French situation reports were regularly twenty-four hours behind the situation.

I was now at about 3,000 feet. The others were forming up on an aircraft in front, but when I got up close I discovered it wasn't Hilly's 'E': it was Peter Boot, who was objecting strongly to everyone forming up on him, but couldn't stop them. There were only six of us now – Hilly and someone else was missing. I had no maps and no clue to our whereabouts, but evidently no one else had either.

I took the lead and searched for an airfield. We saw a town to the south, with a column of grey smoke rising from it to some 4,000 feet spread out at the top like a giant toadstool. I gave it a wide berth, and after zig-zagging about we saw an airfield not far from the town where we'd been shot up. A couple of burnt-out Potez 63s lay in bomb craters on it – and lo and behold, there was a Hurricane taxiing in. I went in to land, and as I touched down I spotted Hilly's 'E' on the Hurricane. Suddenly it swung into wind and took off hastily. I opened my throttle and took straight off again without stopping my run. We formed up and followed Hilly south-east.

Hilly told us later that a Frenchman had sprinted up to him on the ground and shouted 'Get out quick! The Germans are at St Quentin and will be here any minute!' Hilly had also suspected the flak to be German. He had seen the Potez's bombing, and his suspicions had been endorsed by the presence of a Henschel 126 (German army cooperation aircraft), which he had literally blown out of the sky.

We had been using weak mixture for some time, but were very short of petrol when at last we reached Plievaulx, 139 Squadron's airfield. There were no bombers there, but we saw petrol tankers and landed. The CO, Wing Commander Dickens, came over and showed us where to refuel. The tankers were empty, but 139's troops set-to refuelling us from four-gallon drums. We lay on the grass, some of us dozing. I asked Dickens about my old school friend, Tommy Turnbull, and he told me he was all right and had left half an hour earlier for home in one of the Squadron's three remaining Blenheims. He said he'd lost most of his pilots and the Squadron was now recalled to England to re-form. He looked strained and exhausted, and when he mentioned his pilots he spoke with great sadness and looked at the sky. I felt very sorry for him – it must be bloody to be a CO and have to watch your boys go off and be killed one by one, and to have to go on ordering them to do it.

As we talked a smart staff car rolled up, and who should step out but the AOC in person, Air Vice-Marshal Playfair, wearing one of the new officers' field service caps and a perplexed expression. He buttonholed me and asked 'Are you in command of these Hurricanes?' I said 'No, sir, Flying Officer Brown,' and pointed to Hilly. We gathered round while Playfair asked what we were up to. Hilly told him.

'I see,' said Playfair reflectively. 'Yes, it's possible the Germans *are* at St Quentin, although they are not reported there yet.' He knew nothing about our mission to Amiens and went off to telephone AHQ, returning a few minutes later to say we were to refuel and to get on with it, as it was important. He then left, wishing us luck. However, by the time we were refuelled it was much too late in the day to continue, and with a sense of some relief we touched down in the twilight on our stubble-patch at Anglure. Sergeant Albonico was the missing pilot. He was later reported a prisoner of war.

We left the airfield in darkness at ten-thirty and went to dine at a little café the Bull had found in the village. We all crowded in and mechanically shoved down eggs, bread and wine. It might just as well have been sawdust. I made a nuisance of myself by cross-examining the boys for my diary notes. No one cared about diaries or records now – I didn't really care either, but did it from force of habit. I sat on after the others had left, drinking cognac I didn't want with a French air-gunner and trying to be bright with the barmaid. She was quite pretty in a coquettish way, but I could scarcely be bothered to look at a woman these days. At midnight I dragged myself to my feet and shook hands with the Frenchman. We wished each other the luck we knew we needed. He was killed the next day.

The village was crowded-out with *Armée de l'Air* personnel so we made our encampment under pine trees in the grounds of a neighbouring château. The moon was waxing, and the château stood lifeless and staring sightlessly at the black woods. My batman had kindly made my bed in the one and only tent, so I had to sleep in it. Most of the boys dossed down in the soft leaves under the stars.

We knew there was an early start for us in the morning. In the cafe, in camera, we had chewed over our latest assignment. Obviously the Germans were not being held on the ground. Tomorrow the RAF in France and the *Armée de l'Air* were sending over all the bombers they could muster to bomb the German crossings on the river Aisne. Our bombers were to be reinforced from England and covered by all three AASF fighter squadrons. The fighters were to cover the target in succession for a quarter of an hour apiece. 1 Squadron was to be last, which was expected to be the hottest period; the other two, 73 and 501, would be first and second respectively. The success of this bombing raid was considered to be vital. We were to stand by half an hour before dawn.

I could not sleep that night, which was unusual for me. The others were restless too, tossing about, muttering, perhaps dreaming of the morning's job. We were all so completely exhausted that we couldn't relax. Eventually I sank into dreamland – or nightmareland, as it was nowadays.

We were up again at two AM, staggering about groping for our tunics in the dark. Our bodies must be crawling by now, I thought, for we hadn't taken off more than our sweaty tunics for ten days, and we'd slept in all sorts of unlikely places. We piled silently into the transport and drove off to the airfield. We knew it was cold because it always was, but we couldn't feel it; only that trembling in the stomach that made one weak and slightly nauseated.

On the airfield we lay round the base of a haystack to wait for dawn and the order to take off. We waited, but no order came. It was one of the loveliest dawns I have ever seen; I lay still in the hay and watched it. By the time the sun appeared on the horizon the order to take off still hadn't come. We grew restless and fidgeted uneasily. Waiting was bad for us: it strung us up. We weren't used to being given orders to brood on all night, and then hour by hour next day; we were trained to carry out an order on the spot and in double-quick time.

Exasperated, I jumped up and wandered over to my Hurricane. The Bull's parachute was in it, as he wasn't going on this trip, and we were short of packed parachutes for obvious reasons. Thank God we had a splendid parachute-packer – a little Irishman. It had been the peace-time custom to tip our packer ten shillings in the unusual event of making a jump. Now we tipped him a hundred francs a time, so he was waxing rich. I spent an hour pottering about my Hurricane, checking this and that and altering the parachute harness to fit as tightly as possible. I'd learnt the lesson of having a loose harness on my first jump, when I got such a wrench in the groin I thought I'd been shot there.

I went unwillingly back to the hay, longing for some sort of diversion. I tried to sleep, but couldn't, and kept frizzling over the forthcoming trip. I had never felt like this before and I didn't like it. I thought I was losing my nerve and that my morale was low. From previous experience I thought some food might help. I tried to sleep again; no good. I lectured myself severely and called myself a yellow dog. In reply I confessed that I was afraid. I told myself that fear was inadmissible. I answered that it was there regardless. 'All right,' I said to myself, 'get it under control!' I knew all this backwards, but it was therapeutic to go over it again.

I fell to contemplating the quality of courage as it applied to us. I was often afraid before a job, and though none of us admitted it, I knew we all felt the same. Once in the cockpit, though, strapping in, switching on petrol, checking oxygen, starting the engine and checking instruments, the fear turned to the tension of excitement, which was subjugated in its turn by the concentration needed to take off and join up in the air. From then on there was no time to think of anything but finding the enemy, searching every cubic inch of air, and seeing him before he saw me. When I did see him, all the tension and concentration in my body focused in a wild leap of my heart, a flicking-over in the pit of my stomach. It always made me swallow hard a couple of times. After that it was a simple matter: sights switched on, range and wing-span indicators checked, gun button on 'fire', a quick look at the engine instruments and altimeter, an adjustment on the propeller control.

Of course we normally flew with most of these things ready, and sometimes there was no time for fiddling about, but usually we had a few seconds while manoeuvring for position. Then into action, body taut against the straps, teeth clenched, thumb on the gun-button, narrowed eyes intent on getting that black-crossed Hun in the sights and holding him there. I felt my pounding heart turn to a block of ice. Not in fear. My brain became coldly clear, and in an instant I was transformed into a cool, calculating killer. You'd think an aerial combat was a hot-blooded, thrilling affair. It isn't. I've never felt a fighter in a fight – except perhaps in the moment of victory, when I experienced a savage, primitive exaltation. It's not very edifying . . .

Thank heaven breakfast arrived: bread, bully-beef and hot tea. We didn't touch the beef, but drank that tea in a trice, then lay back on the hay refreshed. And yet I could see the boys were still jumpy. It was absurd, but I solemnly cursed the unfortunate staff officer who had given us our orders, apparently quite unnecessarily, the previous night. For the next two hours I was continually troubled by something proclaiming itself as a premonition. I moped about kicking things and throwing stones aimlessly, much to Killy's annoyance. 'For Christ's sake Paul, keep still will you!' he shouted.

At last, at ten o'clock, after a wait of seven-and-a-half hours, the order to take off came through. We doubled across to our machines. It was the first time I'd seen Johnny looking so taut, or any of the boys for that matter. I threw my tin hat and respirator on the ground beside my Hurricane and climbed in. In a few minutes we were off and formed up. This was the first time we had operated as a complete squadron, and I couldn't help wondering whether our present orders had anything to do with my suggestions to Bill Williams a few days earlier. Anyway, we would be able to assess the moral effect of numbers on our own side for once.

As we climbed up through four-tenths of cumulus cloud at 12,000 feet I saw five unescorted Heinkels, in close formation, crossing above and ahead of us from right to left, and called Johnny up to tell him. It broke our hearts to have to leave them alone, but we had to and that was that. Shortly afterwards Hilly, who was Arse-end Charlie with Soper, shouted: 'Look out! They're behind us! Behind us!' We turned individually in a circle, then Hilly called: 'All serene –

they're going away.' We closed up again and resumed our climb.

We reached the patrol line at 20,000 feet and spent our time there getting a little extra height. Now and then we caught sight of formations in the distance, but saw none near us. Under the scattered clouds below there was a slight haze, and we couldn't see our bombers at all.

When our allotted time was up Johnny turned us for home, and we started diving gently but quite fast. At 16,000 feet we suddenly spotted a formation of twenty-five Blenheims below us, going the same way. They were just under the cloudbase at 12,000 feet, and we cheered at the sight. Someone called up 'Good show! There they go!' Yes, it was a good show: it was nice to see some British bombers for a change. They looked strong, deadly and brave in their fine compact formation. We came down behind them in a series of S-turns in close formation, smiling to ourselves. We intended to escort them back to base, or, at any rate, as far as we could.

As we came down closer and examined them in detail as they slid along steadily, in and out of the small clouds, we began to think there was something fishy about those Blenheims. Suddenly Johnny ordered: 'Echelon starboard – Echelon starboard – Go! They're bloody Heinkels!'

We could now see the black crosses on their gunmetal-grey wings. I was No 3 in 'A' flight, i.e. on Johnny's left, and I slid underneath him to come up on Hilly's right in echelon starboard. This was the first formation attack we'd had a chance of making, and the first unescorted bombers we'd come across. Twenty-five Heinkels versus a squadron of Hurricanes! Nice work! Now perhaps we'd be able to dish out a decent dose of their own medicine to the bombers.

We went in astern of them in good formation, Johnny taking the left-hand aircraft of the enemy formation, Hilly the second, and myself the third, leaving Yellow Section of 'A' Flight to come up on our right. We'd practised this attack dozens of times in peacetime, and it almost seemed like practice now, except that the Hun rear-gunners were shooting. The Huns had closed up into sub-formations of threes in Vic, some having a fourth 'in the box' (i.e. below and behind the leader of three). The sub-formations were stepped down and spread out from the leading formation, which consisted of one Vic of three, and each sub-formation appeared to be covering another one with its fire. Their formation was most impressive.

As we went in, steadily closing the range and holding our fire, the smoke of the Huns' tracer bullets snaked through the air towards us. Remorselessly closing in, I was tempted almost to pity the German bombers – but clearly they weren't feeling sorry for us, for the fire got hotter. I was coming up behind the left-hand aircraft of a sub-formation of four Heinkels when I noticed with considerable uneasiness that I seemed to be the focal point of a lot of tracer-lines. At that point I showed poor discipline, but good sense, by swerving slightly to a position astern of the right-hand aircraft of the sub-formation. Just then Soper called out: 'Look out behind! Behind you!' and before we had even fired a shot we broke up, thinking fighters were attacking us from the rear. (It was ascertained afterwards that a Hurricane got in Soper's sights as he was about to fire, and I think it must have been me, but shouting over the R/T was damned stupid, and surprising in a pilot of Soper's experience.)

That wrecked our chance for a formation attack, and the fight recommenced on a basis of individual attacks. This was all the more unfortunate because the German formation were using 'fire control' (a 'fire controller' in one aircraft, usually the leader's, directs all the rear-gunners to fire at one particular enemy aircraft, so that they can concentrate as a group on one). Obviously the most effective counter to fire control was a simultaneous attack by as many fighters as possible, and this was best achieved in some sort of formation.

I had pulled away above, to the right of the Heinkels, to get out of their effective range. As I decided which one to go for, I saw several drop out of formation with Hurricanes firing astern of them, two with their engines smoking and a third with its wheels down. I dived left and turned right again to come up astern of a Hun who had dropped back in the middle of the formation. I was closing and just about to open fire when I heard Hilly shout: 'Behind you! Behind you! Watch out for Christ's sake!' I pulled up to the right and saw another Hurricane pulling away violently to the left. Then I saw what Hilly had been shouting about – and I was glad he had! A damaged Heinkel had dropped astern but had somehow managed to pull himself together again. He had been belting along flat-out behind me; he would probably have got me but for Hilly's warning. I heard Hilly say 'The bastard!' and saw his Hurricane attack the Heinkel, which I think went down. I thought the Hun had put up rather a good show and was sorry in a way to see him go, but thanks Hilly!

I tried again. I went in astern of the extreme right-hand Heinkel of a rear sub-formation of three, fired several bursts and was closing fast when I got in the Heinkel's slipstream and my sights came off. I was nearly on top of him, and judging by the way he suddenly lost speed I must have damaged his engines. I pulled out quickly to the left and turned in on him again, steeply banked to the right, to fire a good deflection burst into his front cockpit. I pulled away to his right, banked smartly left and saw him do a sort of cartwheel, quarter-rolling to the right and dropping his nose simultaneously to the vertical. He went straight into a vertical spiral, and though I saw no smoke or flames, I think he'd had it – heavy bombers don't do that for fun. Probably the pilot was dead or wounded; anyway he was out of the formation.

I now took a quick look round and saw only one Hurricane still with us. I'd been rather long-winded and presumed most of 'A' Flight had run out of ammunition and gone home. I still had plenty left, and went in astern of a lagging Heinkel on the left of the formation. Just as I was closing, a dense clump of flak exploded in the rear of the formation, extending all around me. I glanced left and saw the other Hurricane similarly surrounded with bursts but pressing straight on. A shell burst just beneath me and I heard a muffled bang as an assortment of bits came up through my port wing. The aircraft jerked from the shock, but I wasn't going to lose that seductively lagging Heinkel, and kept on after him. He was flat-out to catch up, and had nearly made it, when I had him in range and opened fire.

Between bursts I noticed I was drawing a hell of a lot of cross-fire from the formation. I heard several pops and saw more holes appear in both my wings. I was astonished to hear a loud bang as a cannon-shell opened a decent-sized hole in my port wing. Tough, these boys! But I was surprised how calm I felt, and how coolly I was thinking. I remember making a mental note of that rear cannon, and thinking that these Heinkels must be Mark Vs. Suddenly smoke belched from both my Heinkel's engines, his wheels dropped and he went down in a shallow right-hand diving turn. I let him go and pulled up left.

I still had about a hundred rounds to each gun left, I judged, and

I was excited to see a Heinkel swerve and break formation as a clump of flak burst in his sub-formation. He dropped back below the formation, but immediately regained control and opened up to full throttle to catch up. But he'd lost a couple of hundred yards, and naturally I pounced, going in astern and opening fire almost straightaway. I noted another sub-formation of three, with one in the box, ahead and above right, throwing everything they had at me.

I concentrated on my Heinkel. I had him beautifully steady in the sights and poured short savage bursts into him as I closed. I was wondering why he showed no sign of being hit, because I knew I was hitting him. He had nearly caught his formation up when grey smoke streamed from both his engines, then from his wing-roots and fuselage, and in a second he was completely enveloped. I felt that savage thrill again and said: 'And that for luck, you sod!' as I fired a final burst into the burning mass. It was only half a burst, because I ran out of ammunition with a hiss of compressed air. As I broke lazily away to the left, feeling pretty pleased with myself, I glanced at the still-firing sub-formation and mentally put two fingers up in derision. It was then I learnt a lesson I should have known and will never forget.

Just as I rolled – too slowly – over to the left to dive away, I saw a sudden flash of tracer very close, and in the same second heard several pops, then a deafening 'Bang!' in my right ear. (I think it came from the boys above right, but it's just possible that the rear gunner of the blazing Heinkel was still firing, and if so I raise my hat yet again!) In that instant I knew they'd hit my aeroplane. A shower of blood spurted down my right side. My Hurricane was diving almost vertically, and I was surprised to see my right arm, drenched in blood, raised up in front of me against the hood. There was no feeling in it – the hand was hooked like a dead bird's claw. All this happened in a flash; but so quickly does the mind work that in the same moment I guessed at and assessed the damage and decided how to act. That 'Bang!' still echoed in my right ear, and I said aloud 'Cannon shell in right shoulder – arm may be almost severed – write that off – pull out of dive with left hand, and if necessary bale out, pulling ripcord with left hand.'

But to my horror I found my left arm wouldn't move either! It hung limp and straight down my side. I looked up to find the aircraft plunging earthwards out of control; it was repeatedly diving, gaining speed, flattening out, losing speed and diving again. I had the extraordinary sensation of my head being isolated from the rest of my body inside the cockpit. I was perfectly conscious and could hear the hiss of the airflow rise and fall over the cockpit roof. I looked at my inert body and tried with all my strength to move my arms. My right hand, or claw, was within four inches of the hood handle, but strain as I might I couldn't get it any nearer. The ground was coming up; I could hear myself grunting and straining to move. Then suddenly I heard myself scream. Muffled but clearly audible, I heard myself mutter it, then say it, then shout it: 'God! God! I'm going to be killed! God!'

I stopped shouting abruptly and looked into the bottom of the cockpit, thinking 'I won't feel it!' I looked up again and saw the ground rushing up now – and suddenly my left arm moved. So obsessed had I become with the idea of escape that my hand flew to the hood handle to pull it back. It was jammed! I heaved frantically with the manic strength of desperation, but it didn't budge an inch. I looked again into the cockpit, frightened of fire. Then my right hand suddenly flopped on to the stick, pulled it back, and out of that hellish dive I came. None too soon either, though not desperately low – at about 2,000 feet, to be exact.

I chattered away to myself: 'My God! That's the narrowest squeak I ever want! Now get down smartly – you may be on fire – and your engine's stopped'. I glanced over the instruments and noticed the air-speed indicator wasn't registering at all – a bullet or shell must have got the pitot head or some part of the airspeed-indicator system. I had lots of holes in my wings, and a bullet-hole in the windscreen to the right of the bullet-proof section. I wondered where the bullet had gone . . .

I was beginning to feel severe pain in the right side of my neck and face, and thought a cannon shell had struck the side of the cockpit and blown a chunk out of me. I still couldn't get the hood open. I circled as I glided down, picked a field near a village so that I could get help quickly, pumped my flaps down and went in to land with my wheels up. As I held off over a harrowed field I braced myself with my left hand against the sight bar. We touched, bounced and bucketed across the field, grinding along in a cloud of dust. Blood splashed over the dashboard and windscreen. Then, just as I thought we were going over, the tail came down with a thump and we came to rest.

I whipped the pin out of my Sutton harness, unclipped my parachute and tried to open the hood. It was still stuck firm, so I jammed both feet against the instrument panel and tugged. No: it wouldn't move. My neck and shoulder throbbed and I was feeling weak, so I rested a moment. From the bottom of the cockpit little wisps of smoke or dust – I wasn't sure which – were rising. I seized the hood-handles once more, heaving and straining with all my remaining strength, but the thing held stubbornly firm and I had to rest again. This was bloody! It looked as though I had escaped a comparatively pleasant death by diving into the ground only to be burnt alive. I wondered if the first lick of flame would give me the strength to bust out of this damned cockpit, or, if not, whether death would come quickly in the heat and smoke. Once again I redoubled my efforts: no good. The emergency panel would not come out with the hood closed, but I bashed out the small break-out panel in the left side of the hood with my fist and put my arm through it, for no reason other than to have access to the outside world.

Why the hell didn't those bloody Frenchmen get a move on? I could hear something dripping and smelt petrol. This galvanized me into one final effort – and suddenly, with a jerk, the hood came half-open. I hauled myself out on to the starboard wing and ran away from the aeroplane, expecting an explosion. Panting and exhausted, I stumbled towards a wooded stream. Then I stopped and looked back. No sign of smoke or fire. I went slowly back. I noticed odd things, such as the quiet and the heat, very clearly; others, such as the holes in my aircraft, not at all. Presumably a bullet had damaged the hood runners, but I forgot to look. I stood on the wing and leaned into the cockpit, switching off the reflector sight, turning off the petrol and main engine switches, putting the gun button to 'Safe', and taking out my maps, all in a methodical and automatic way. I walked round to the other side, carrying my helmet and maps. I was getting a good deal of pain now and was staggering. I kicked in the panel where the first-aid kit was kept to get at the morphia; but it was a new aeroplane from England and they hadn't bothered to put in the first-aid kit. I swore graphically, then told myself not to be a bloody sissy, that I only had a minor flesh wound in the neck anyway.

All the same, it hurt. I had no idea at the time, but I had been shot in the neck by an armour-piercing bullet. It nicked the angle of my jaw in entering, exposed the carotid artery and lodged against the front of the spine at the base of the neck. The shock to the spine had caused temporary paralysis. A little more pressure, and the paralysis would have been permanent – that is, until I hit the ground. A fraction of a millimetre to one side and I would have bled to death from a sev-ered carotid within minutes. A little less height and I would have dived in. A fire, or an uncontrollable aircraft, and I couldn't have baled out. A little more or a little less of this or that – but what the hell? I was just lucky.

At last two French soldiers hailed me a couple of fields away, their rifles trained on me. I put up my hands but was too weak to hold them high, and they fell to my shoulders. The Frenchmen, advancing slowly, stopped and took aim again. I put my arms up once more, but couldn't make it and collapsed panting, with everything swim-ming. I staggered to my feet again, and mercifully two cars arrived with a screech and out jumped a French officer and some soldiers. They ran towards me, pointing revolvers, and seeing their small new-issue helmets I thought they were Germans. They surrounded me as I mumbled *'Je suis anglais – regardez mon avion!'* The kindly officer helped me to the car, saying in a distressed voice: *'Oh mon pauvre, mon pauvre!'* He told me he had watched me coming down, and had seen me shoot down my last Heinkel. *'Le voilà!'* he said, pointing to a column of smoke rising behind some trees. I said I thought I had got two others in the fight and he immediately broadcast the news triumphantly, and his men looked at me as if I were some sort of superman. I certainly felt anything but at the time, and my feelings weren't improved by a bearded *poilu* who, much to the officer's fury, took a good look at my neck and stammered: *'Diable! Il a tout le côté ouvert!'*

They drove me at breakneck speed to a French hospital at La Ferté-sous-Jouarre, not far from Château-Thierry, where I was briefly examined, had a dressing slapped on and a shot of anti-tetanus in the leg. I was then shoved into an ancient ambulance on a stretcher and whizzed off to another hospital eighty kilometres west, as this one was evacuating. They refused me morphia for some reason, so I just had to lie clinging to a rail with my left hand and stick it for four or five hours while the ambulance jolted and lurched along.

'*Il a l'air de souffrir,*' said one of the nursing orderlies. True, no doubt. '*Il est choqué,*' said the other, which was fortunately also true. I have experienced no greater pain in my life, though doubtless others have. I felt it could get no worse, and that if it did, I couldn't stick it. But I knew I *could* stick it because I jolly well had to.

Eventually, after bumping along country lanes and reversing into fields, the driver confessed he couldn't find the hospital. I rallied enough to order him to take me to the American Hospital in Paris, twenty-five kilometres away. As each sentry challenged us, the driver shouted: '*Aviateur anglais! Il a descendu trois Boches!*' and he repeated this announcement to every policeman and bystander as he asked the way. When we finally arrived at the American Hospital at Neuilly, the driver jumped down with his '*Aviateur anglais! Il a descendu trois Boches!*' and asked if they would take me.

I heard a young woman with an American accent say: '*Ils ont du courage, vous savez!*' and smiled to myself, but found a certain comfort in her words. I tried to get up and walk into the hospital, as I felt damned silly lying down like that, but I was pressed back gently and relaxed gratefully. As I was carried out of the bright sunlight into the cool darkness inside, a vision with blonde hair in the uniform of the American Ambulance Corps pressed my hand, in which I still clutched my blood-stained flying helmet, and said: 'It's going to be all right!' I thought she had the sweetest voice I had ever heard and was more beautiful than anyone I had ever seen. My eyes filled with sudden tears, and all I could manage in return was a twisted smile of gratitude as I thought fervently 'God bless America!'

XV
PARIS IN SPRINGTIME

Doc Rogers came straight to see me. He had been a great friend of the Squadron at Etretat, near Havre, at the beginning of the war. I asked him to ring the British Embassy to inform the Squadron that I was OK and that I thought I had shot down three Heinkels. The message got no further than British Air Forces in France HQ at Coulommiers, and poor old Hilly spent two long days searching French hospitals for me. Professor de Martel, the celebrated neurosurgeon, assisted by Rogers, removed the bullet two hours after my admission. Sally, a pretty young American nurse, very sweetly held my hand until I went under. For thirty hours after coming round I vomited at half-hourly intervals – a most painful performance. Not having had a drink since early on the morning of the fight, I was mad with thirst, but I couldn't drink. I suppose I was delirious: the vision of that dive kept recurring and I heard myself shouting again and again: 'God! I'm going to be killed!' This would promptly make me throw up again. It wasn't much fun.

With the excellent attention I received I made a rapid recovery. The operation was on Sunday, 19 May. The following Sunday, 26 May, I was propped up, bearded and sore, but happy, when who should turn up but Lewis and Soper, the latter with a well-deserved flight-sergeant's crown on his sleeve. Soon Johnny, Boy, Prosser, Stratters and Killy burst in. They were all on their way home to England, having been relieved, and were in terrific spirits.

'Well you silly old bugger!' Johnny said. 'How the hell did you make such a mess of yourself? Bloody good show anyway!' He told me the fight on 19 May had been the Squadron's last of any note.

Soper said he had shot down a couple of Heinkels in the fight when one of his wing fuel tanks was hit by an incendiary bullet and caught fire. He dived so fast he blew the fire out, then forced-landed near Château-Thierry. He went into the nearest town to pick up some transport, but no one was interested in a British pilot on foot. Shortly afterwards the Germans gave the town a thorough pasting and Soper saw some French soldiers in a panic throwing women and children out of air-raid shelters to get in themselves. He then saw the said women and children blown to bits, arms and legs and chunks of flesh flying all over the place. To round the scene off, the hospital, clearly marked with red crosses on its roof, was deliberately destroyed by Stukas.

Johnny said we only got eight Heinkels in the fight, which we didn't think was much good. He added that he and the boys were going back to England to form a fighter school under the Bull, who had already left, and Air Ministry hoped they would be in time to give the untried Fighter Command squadrons some tips and pass on the experience we had gained before the Germans attacked Britain. He ended by telling me that I was to join them when I was fit. But in my heart of hearts I still hoped I could rejoin the re-formed Squadron. I little realized I was not to be able to fly again for six months, and not to be fit to fight again for a further five.

After the boys left I fell to reviewing the events of the past months. The last few days made previous experiences seem unreal. Those ten days of concentrated fighting, from 10 May to 19 May, seemed shrouded in fog now. Lying there quietly between cool white sheets, my sweaty and verminous uniform now clean and draped on a chair, I had only the hole in my neck to remind me that it had all really happened. But the Squadron's record to date was clear enough, and I totted it up from my notes, which Donald Hills had brought with my kit; 30 October 1939–9 May 1940: 26 enemy aircraft destroyed; our losses: one new pilot; 10–19 May 1940: 114 enemy aircraft destroyed; our losses: two pilots presumed killed, two wounded, one prisoner of war. It seemed – and I believe it was – a miracle.

Soon I was moved into a room with a French captain who had been blinded. He was a nice chap and we got on famously. We used to listen to the *bulletins d'information* on his wireless. Things weren't looking too bright, but I thought the Frenchman right when he said

'*On se débrouillera.*' Doc Rogers often looked in on us when he had time. He thought the news depressing; but the German push from Sedan had swept through the Champagne district and then turned away from Paris in a north-westerly direction. It was now making for the Channel ports. Everyone said Paris was well defended. 'And I have great faith in the French Army,' said the Doc, voicing our feelings in the matter.

A lot of wounded were now arriving from that same army. They were mainly head cases for Professor de Martel. Several of the poor devils were insane, and their shrieks and moans echoed down the long hospital corridors; I have never heard such a blood-curdling or utterly hopeless sound. But Doc Rogers said it was surprising how many eventually recovered – eighty per cent, I think he estimated. There was only one airman in the place besides myself – a Frenchman who was severely burnt – and no other British wounded.

A fortnight passed and I insisted on getting up. I had lost fifteen pounds and felt idiotically weak, but I wanted to regain my strength as quickly as possible and get back to the Squadron. I couldn't turn my neck, and the trapezius muscle in my right shoulder wasn't functioning because the nerve was destroyed. However, it was fun to be up and about again, pottering in the garden or sitting on the roof.

Once I watched de Martel operate. A piece of skull about four inches square had been removed, and the great surgeon probed and delicately incised the brain with his marvellously steady hands. He produced a shell splinter with 'Look now, Monsieur! Look well now!' The patient started yelling and I felt suddenly faint and had to go outside. Doc Rogers came with me, laughing. He said: 'I'm glad to see that. I don't feel so inadequate now!' I asked what he meant, and he replied, 'Well, we couldn't face the things you do up there, like diving at four or five hundred miles an hour, and it makes me feel better to find that you can't face what *we* can down here!'

I often wanted to express my admiration for the work of the hospital staff. They were mostly Americans, with a couple of French doctors, and French, Danish, Dutch, Swiss, Swedish and English nurses. Now that the wounded were coming in, de Martel and Rogers operated day after day continuously from seven in the morning until four the following one. The other doctors were just as indefatigable, and the nurses never lacked courage, energy or good humour. I thought they were all magnificent, and I am forever indebted to them for their kindness to me.

Came Dunkirk. For the small but valiant British Army penned against the sea there seemed little hope. Of only one thing were we certain: they would fight to the end. They did – and to a better end than anyone expected. The surrender of King Leopold of the Belgians was a sad blow, but in spite of Reynaud's violent denunciation a lot of people felt there was more to the affair than met the eye, and that, as Churchill had said, no one could judge yet.

Several French friends visited me in hospital. One of the first was Gilonne d'Origny*, who asked permission to take me to lunch in a nearby restaurant. Another was Emeline Castéja and her husband Alec, who took me to lunch in the *Bois* with one of the Princesses de Caraman-Chimay. The latter was a relative of the King of the Belgians, and she declared that she was now ashamed of her nationality. And June Bowman, a delightful English girl, often took me out in her car.

Count Alec Castéja had been in what was the *Ier Chasseurs-à-Cheval*, now a light mechanized regiment. He was in the fighting round Sedan. His unit was with the Second Army, next to General Corap's Ninth Army, and with other French light units had been sent out in front of the main forces on 10 May. Their role was to hold the Germans off for at least twenty-six hours and then retire to the main fortifications. Alec said the light units of the Second Army, and those of the First Army (placed on the other side of the Ninth), had held the Germans for forty-eight hours, and hoped to continue to do so. But the centrally placed Ninth Army had suddenly retired under General Corap's orders. Alec said the Ninth Army's Senegalese troops had been unable to take more than eight hours' continuous dive-bombing and had broken. Scarcely surprising, I thought . . .That was how the Germans got through, said Alec, aided by treachery that included the murder of senior

---

*Daughter of Comte Pierre de Jannel de Vauréal, the Vicomtesse d'Origny spent the rest of the war in France as an intelligence officer, became a captain in the *Forces Françaises Indépendantes*, was made an Officer of the *Légion d'Honneur* and was awarded the *Croix de Guerre* with Palm and the *Médaille de la Résistance*.

French officers outside their quarters and the poisoning of key men.

The Ninth Army consisted largely of reservists because its position behind the Ardennes Forest was considered impassable by tanks. It wasn't. Once through, said Alec, the Germans had fanned out behind the flanking armies, spreading alarmist and defeatist rumours with the aid of fifth-columnists – 'The Germans are behind you!' etc – but otherwise doing little damage. The flanking forces fell back hurriedly in some confusion, vainly trying to re-establish a line, while the high-speed *Panzers* raced on unopposed. The French were well but insufficiently equipped. They had no mobile reserves, their front-line armies were not flexible enough, and the generals were continually trying to re-establish a line somewhere.

This 'line complex' was shared by the general public and ordinary soldiers such as myself. A senior French Army officer once told the Squadron, 'If the Germans succeed in crossing the Meuse we'll hold the line of the Marne; if necessary we'll retire to the Seine, and then even to the Loire.' It began to look as though we might have to . . . But we were always looking for a line.

On 3 June, just before lunch, the Paris sirens wailed. I was chatting with Doc Rogers downstairs, and hearing anti-aircraft fire we took the lift to the roof. The firing was heavy and we could hear the engines of many aeroplanes. 'So here it is!' said Rogers, as we stood beneath a small concrete shelter to avoid shell fragments. There was a terrible row going on – bangs, crumps and whistles and the clatter of fragments. I stepped out and stared up through the heat haze: I could hear them all right, but only saw two bombers and the sun-flash of an escorting fighter between the fluffy clouds. Great billows of black and grey smoke were rolling across the city, from St Denis, the Seine and St Germain to the west. In about twenty minutes the last of the bombers had droned away to the accompaniment of rattling machine-gun fire from French fighters. We looked at the smoke and dust-laden air, and then at each other, and grinned sheepishly.

'I'm glad we painted out our red crosses!' said Rogers as we went down to lunch.

'Berlin tonight . . .' I said. I hoped I was right.

An *Armée de l'Air* friend later told me the Huns had used a hundred and fifty bombers and about two hundred fighters on this raid.

The French shot down seventeen – mostly on their return trip – which was not too brilliant even if there were few French fighter squadrons based round Paris. Two hundred and fifty-seven people were killed in Paris, and the worst damage was to the Citroen works, the aerodromes round the city and the French Air Ministry. The raid appeared to be a legitimate one directed at military objectives, though the bombing was not all accurate, probably owing to conditions of visibility. It certainly was a well-calculated psychological stroke.

Perhaps I had got up too soon, for I suddenly developed a temperature and went back to bed for two days feeling rotten. More and more French wounded were flooding in, and the hospital staff was working flat-out. Several women ambulance drivers were shot up by Hun aircraft, and one drove back pluckily with a bullet in her buttock. Ambulances disappeared without trace and were presumed casualties. The Huns seemed to be deliberately strafing vehicles marked with red crosses, and the hospital authorities ordered them to be erased.

A French tank captain was brought in. He told me his tank had knocked out four Hun tanks before finishing up locked head-on with a fifth, both of them catching fire. He said the French tanks were superior to the German, but were heavily outnumbered. He also said the Huns were spread-eagling prisoners on the fronts of their tanks and using them as rams or collision mats*. A French doctor said he had attended many German prisoners and considered their hyper-excited condition could only be attributed to the use of drugs. This applied particularly to the airmen. I discounted this, knowing the unbalancing effect of strain in air fighting, and especially of being shot down. But if he was right, would it explain the Germans' fatalistic method of mass attack, seen both in the air and on the ground? Would it explain that split-second superiority in reaction that we ourselves had invariably found we had over the Huns in combat? †

On 5 June I asked permission to become an outpatient to vacate a much-needed bed. Walter Wylie, a friend of mine in the American Embassy, asked me to stay at his flat. I spent the next few days

*I have never heard this story corroborated, though doubtless SS units were capable of it.

†It was later established that German airmen did not take drugs. Mass attack is a German tradition and our own superiority in reaction must be attributed to training and experience.

unwisely but happily, bathing and lying in the sun at the Racing Club in the *Bois*, teetering about from café to restaurant, restaurant to bar, eating, drinking and spending too much, but rejoicing in, and never so grateful for, being alive. Paris retained its irresponsible gaiety. Couples still drank champagne and sang romantic choruses in boulevard cafés. Albert still bowed one in with a portly gesture and a welcoming smile at Maxim's. The Ritz Bar was still in full swing before lunch and dinner. The only noticeable change was the almost total absence of soldiers.

I walked down the *Champs Elysées* towards the *Concorde* one afternoon and stumbled across Cobber Kain sitting at a pavement table with Noel Monks, air correspondent of the *Daily Mail*. Over a drink Cobber told me the rest of the original 73 Squadron had gone back to England and that the Squadron had been re-formed. He had stayed behind to help get things going, but was off in a couple of days. He was on a few hours' leave. He said they'd had some losses – five killed and several wounded, I think – and told me his personal score of Huns was seventeen. I noticed that he was nervous and preoccupied, and kept breaking matches savagely in one hand while he glowered into the middle distance. Like the rest of us, he'd had enough for a while.

Next day a Hurricane roared down and beat up 73's airfield southwest of Paris. To finish off, it did a couple of flick-rolls in succession at 200 feet and foolishly attempted a third with insufficient speed. It spun off, straightened out promptly enough, but had no height and went straight in. The rescue squad was shocked to find an identity disc marked 'Flying Officer E. J. Kain' on the pilot's body. So died a great Cobber.

The night after the Paris raid I had wandered along to the APNA (the French professional aviators' club) in the *Avenue Kléber*. Usually it was an extremely cheerful spot, but that night there was an intolerable air of gloom about it. I arrived in high spirits and looking forward to a drink with my old friends Fifi Fickinger, Amiot chief test pilot, and Captain Maréchal and Colonel Rosanoff of the French Air Force. But Fifi was propping up the bar alone and very dismal. He sadly told me that Maréchal had been killed in combat with the German bombers over Paris that morning, and that Rosanoff was at the front with a fighter squadron. I retired to bed shortly afterwards, having well and truly caught the general depression.

Fifi and I met for drinks several times thereafter, and on Sunday 9 June he took me to lunch at the *Popote des Ailes*, the French test pilots' mess near Villacoublay. We drove out in his little Simca and found a crowd waiting for us in the bar. Most of France's top professional pilots were there, and I collected their signatures on a menu – one of my favourite souvenirs.

They threw dice to decide who would pay for the lunch, and again for the wine – a daily custom – and then we trooped across a garden into the mess-room. It was well hung with trophies and the walls were covered with signed photographs of past and present members of the mess, which included every well-known pilot France has ever produced. Maurice Claisse, Breguet's chief test pilot, showed me round, pointing out various photographs:

''E was lost in the *Atlantique* . . .' ''E crashed and was killed in Syria . . .' ''Is aeroplane broke up in ze air . . .' ''Is motor cut and 'e spun in at Buc . . .'

Most of them were dead. There was an aura of romance about these professionals, most of them badly scarred from burns and broken bones, the results of their many crashes. They were all gay, reckless and courageous – what we in the RAF call 'regardless' – as only French pilots can be.

Fifi, unlucky at dice, paid for the food; Casanova, the pilot with whom I was shot-up over Arras in October 1939, bought the wine; and *'Mémère'*, the huge rollicking lady who had run the café for 'her' pilots for over twenty years (and only charged them when she knew they could afford it, which was rare), served it up with great panache.

After lunch they sang me a drinking song – an adaptation, for Hitler's benefit, of a song once sung by French sailors and aimed at Queen Anne of England:

'Buvons un coup!
Buvons-en deux!
A la santé des amoureux!
A la santé de notre France!
Et merde *pour ce salaud d'Hitler**
Qui nous a déclaré la guerre!

Pour ceux qui vont périr en mer
Levons nos verres!
Pour ceux qui vont mourir en l'air
Buvons un coup!
Buvons-en deux!'

The proceedings ended abruptly when news came in of a crash at Villacoublay. Everyone left hurriedly, leaving Fifi to return me to Paris.

On the way he spoke about the new Amiot heavy bomber he was testing: with Rolls-Royce Merlin engines he'd got it up to 330 mph at 18,000 feet – very nearly as fast as the Hurricane. He asked me how many Germans I'd shot down, and refused to believe it when I said 'Eight or nine' because I had no decorations!

*Originally 'la reine d'Angleterre'.

XVI

WHO'S FOR CRICKET?

I felt at the time there was an air of finality about that lunch, and that the shadow of the German Army was already spreading ominously over Paris.

A lot of Parisians were on the move, with baggage strapped to their cars and mattresses on the roofs for protection against strafing aircraft. The Germans were making for the capital now, coming up the Seine from Rouen. They were already at Mantes and I couldn't risk staying any longer. Had I known at the time how little stood in their path I should have pushed off long before.

On Monday, 9 June, I packed my kit, said goodbye and a fervent thank-you to the American Hospital, and obtained an *Ordre de Mission* from Squadron Leader Wells, RAF assistant provost marshal, to travel by train to Blois. The Embassy had left, and I was lucky to find out that Headquarters Advanced Air Striking Force was now at Blois from my well-informed chum Larry Le Sueur of the Columbia Broadcasting System, whom I found in the deserted Crillon bar.

I made for the *Gare de Lyon* in an RAF lorry. We couldn't get near the station: it was surrounded by a threshing multitude of people fighting to get in. We tried the *Gare d'Austerlitz*, which was likewise besieged, but succeeded in ploughing a passage through to the platform and a harassed official. He said that the lines were being continually bombed, there was no time-table and the trains were dangerously crammed anyway. So with regret I returned and explained to Wells that he would have to take me with him somehow next morning. Naturally he wasn't too pleased, as he was full up already and it meant that he'd have to make a detour to drop me at

Blois. He had planned to make for Nantes by small byroads to avoid the traffic. However, he accepted the inevitable and told me to be ready at his headquarters at five the next morning. I then went off and bought my wife a hat from a closing-down milliner.

I went back to Walter's flat and tried to relax by playing Tchaikowsky's *Pathétique* Symphony on the gramophone, but it only increased my depression. I went out and wandered about the city in an aimless fashion. The shops and restaurants were boarded up, the streets deserted except for an occasional heavily laden car. An atmosphere of desolation had settled over Paris.

After dark I walked up the *Champs Elysées* to the *Etoile* and stood for some time beneath the *Arc de Triomphe* looking at the tomb of the Unknown Soldier. The light of the flame flickered fitfully up Napoleon's great arches and over the inscription on the stone slab below: *'Ici repose un soldat français, mort pour la patrie.'* A cloaked gendarme loomed out of the darkness and stood beside me: a silent bond linked us.

At five AM on Tuesday, 11 June, we assembled outside the provost marshal's headquarters. It was light, but there was a strange fog over the city; there was also a sickly smell of burning. In the distance we could hear the shaking rumble of heavy gunfire: hell must be popping out there. We were missing one man. We wasted two and a half hours looking for the bloody nuisance before we found him asleep. At last we moved off. Our small convoy consisted of the APM's car, a truck carrying fifteen RAF service policemen and our baggage, and two RAF dispatch-riders on motor-bikes who proved invaluable in getting us through.

We soon reached the open country, but the roads were crammed with cars belting along three and four abreast and the now familiar flotilla of carts, push-bikes and even perambulators. I looked through the rear window for a last time at the deserted city with the shroud-like pall of smoke hanging over it. The smoke persisted for forty miles and came from huge oil dumps fired by the French down the Seine. It dirtied our faces and made the dispatch-riders look like a couple of black men. They were highly competent riders and worked unceasingly at shepherding our convoy along, straightening out traffic jams and generally introducing an air of calm efficiency where previously there had been only a jabbering babel of rapidly rising panic.

At last we arrived at Châteaudun, in whose castle many treasures from the Louvre were stored. We were told an RAF squadron was stationed there and hoped to beg some petrol from them, but we couldn't locate the airfield and proceeded down the road to Blois. If only I had known, 1 Squadron was stationed at Châteaudun! We came to an airfield with Battles parked on it, and were directed to a village where we found 103 Squadron installed. Wing Commander Dickens, their CO*, welcomed us and gave us lunch. When I was told my Squadron was just up the road I decided to drop off. I dumped my kit, complete with my wife's hat, and said farewell to the provost marshal.

I learned from the 103 boys that 75 Wing Headquarters, which had been at Auberive when I lunched there after my second bale-out, was in a nearby château. I decided to retrieve a pistol I had carelessly left with them on the previous occasion, and Dickens kindly provided me with transport later in the afternoon.

Poor old Dickens was very 'bloody minded', for he had lost nearly all his pilots – almost entirely, he said, through having to order them to carry out jobs left undone by the French army. Our old chums 12 Squadron had lost twenty-six complete aircrews – seventy-eight flying personnel – and only six of the original squadron pilots had survived. These Battle and Blenheim boys of the AASF were the real heroes. We fighter chaps had a deadly aeroplane in our hands and had the consolation of hitting back and chalking up a score. But the bombers had none of the thrill, none of the fast aerobatics, and twice the danger. They knew every time they took off that they didn't stand much chance of coming back, but they never shirked a job and never hesitated. We all admired and respected them, and it was our greatest sorrow that we were physically unable to protect them as planned.

Over at 75 Wing, I rescued my gun from Bill Waleran, who was confident he had 'won' it and was somewhat disappointed to see me again! Group Captain Wann, the CO, invited me to stay to dinner, so I sent my transport off and kept my kit with me. Wing's château belonged to the Baron-somebody. I had seen a Dornier with French markings doing a low reconnaissance of it as I arrived, which was disturbing. The baron was in residence, with his English wife and attractive daughter of nineteen, and we all sat down to dinner. I was

*Not the previously mentioned CO of 114 Squadron.

rather embarrassed when Wann – who by the way was the sole sur-
vivor of the airship R 101 when it crashed at Beauvais in 1931 –
referred to me as 'the calmest man in the world' and regaled our
hosts with the story of how I had arrived at Wing one morning by
parachute. I said 'What a line!' to Doc Polson beside me, rather too
loudly, I'm afraid, as Wann shot me a sharp look.

After dinner I got blind drunk with Polson and fell asleep while
the Group Captain was talking to me. But he was a damn' good chap
and I don't think he minded. After a few more drinks Doc Polson
carried me off to bed.

Next morning I rejoined the re-formed 1 Squadron at Châteaudun.
Squadron Leader Pemberton was in command and Hilly was a flight
commander. Sergeant Clowes was still there, and Knackers, as irre-
pressible as ever and keeping everyone's spirits up as he had done
throughout the French campaign.

That night three mysterious civilians arrived at the château to collect all secret documents, which they did after Pemberton had checked
them up by telephone with AHQ. The incredible rumour was that
the French were going to throw in their hand and that the Squadron
was off to Corsica. All non-essential documents were destroyed, and
our kit was packed ready to move at a moment's notice.

On 14 June the Germans goose-stepped into Paris, and that same
day Professor de Martel, having operated on wounded French soldiers twenty-one hours a day for five weeks, took his own life.

On 17 June France asked Germany for an armistice and on 26
June laid down her arms, though part of the French army in eastern
France continued to fight.

1 and 73 Squadrons covered the embarkation of the RAF and the
remains of the BEF at Nantes, and 1 Squadron shot down a further
fifteen Huns, one being the Heinkel that sank the SS *Lancastria* and
cost us 3,000 lives. They left France on 18 June, by which time Hilly
Brown's personal score stood at seventeen and 1 Squadron's at one-
hundred-and-fifty-five enemy aircraft destroyed in France.

Just before the squadron left, Moses Demozay was ordered by his
French superiors to report to a depot in Nantes. Rightly suspecting he
was to be demobilized, he ignored the order and went to the airfield
instead to thumb a lift to England. After being pushed off several

aircraft, he found an abandoned RAF Bristol Bombay twin-engined transport with a broken tailwheel and rudder. Although he had not flown for five years, had never flown a twin, and had no maps, he got a fitter to start the engines and flew the old crate to England with fifteen jubilant RAF troops aboard. As if this was not enough, when he couldn't find an airfield he allowed a sergeant who lived in the Midlands to guide him by railway lines to one near his home town!

I left Châteaudun in a de Havilland Rapide mail-plane on 14 June. We took off in showery weather, circling the bomb-pitted aerodrome littered with destroyed hangars and French aircraft blown on to their backs, then headed north-west for Normandy. Heavy black storm-clouds rolled across the sky, and I hoped no enemy fighters would pop round them, for we had no armament.

Below us, now in rainy shadow, now in mottled sunlight, we could see dense columns of refugees stretched across the green countryside like dirty white ribbons. From every town and every village rose crooked clouds of smoke, and now and then we would catch sight of a stationary train. I had a camera with me and no doubt could have taken some historic photographs; but I somehow felt it was not the moment, as one shrinks from taking pictures of a tragic accident.

Since I had been wounded my capacity for sleep had been prodigious, and I slept now. I woke over the Channel Islands; they were bathed in sunlight and were sharply outlined in a smooth sea. Soon we were crossing the Dorset coast. I looked down on the calm and peaceful English countryside, the smoke rising, not from bombed villages, but lazily from cottage chimneys, and saw a game of cricket in progress on a village pitch. With my mind still filled with the blast and flame that had shattered France, I was seized with utter disgust at the smug insular contentedness England enjoyed behind her sea barrier. I thought a few bombs might wake those cricketers up, and that they wouldn't be long in coming either.

As we glided down on to Hendon aerodrome my emotions were so mixed that I had difficulty in controlling them. I cannot describe them very well – they don't really matter much anyway. I suppose it was a culmination of many things that brought tears to my eyes – something to do with what I had seen, the friends I had left behind, and the almost unbelievable fact that I was home.

APPENDIX I

Author's letter to his parents 4 September 1939

ROYAL AIR FORCE,
TANGMERE,
CHICHESTER,
SUSSEX.

TEL. CHICHESTER 443.
TELEGRAPHIC ADDRESS, AERONAUTICS, CHICHESTER.

4 . 9 . 39

Darling Mum & Dad & Mike.

Sorry I haven't been able to write sooner. Have been on duty continuously for last 48 hours.

Well, the war's started, & we're waiting to deal with any Germans who cross our coasts. As a matter of fact, we thought we'd be attacked & bombed just before dawn this morning. At 12.30 some of us lay us down to rest, but at

2.

3.15 a.m. we took off — in heavy ground-mist but a very clear moon-lit night. However, nothing happened, & we were soon down again. We then awaited the landing of some of our bombers who had been to Germany — five, we were told. At 6.30, one appeared. We were somewhat shaken at the thought of what had happened to the rest! Then came another through the mist. No more. We all turned out to greet the poor blighters — they'd been in the air 8 hours. To my surprise I saw a whole lot of paper

ROYAL AIR FORCE,
TANGMERE,
CHICHESTER,
SUSSEX.

TEL. CHICHESTER 443.
TELEGRAPHIC ADDRESS, AERONAUTICS, CHICHESTER.

3.

struck round the tail - wheel of one —— &
guessed the answer: pamphlets! Flying
largely through heavy cloud, & thickly
covered with ice, they had bombarded
the Ruhr valley with —— paper! It took
3 men, one hour to chuck it out. They
in each aircraft
could see the great blast - furnaces below;
otherwise nothing. very few search - lights or
A.A. fire. Only one fighter —— & he
vanished after a burst from the bomber.
A really fine effort, I think, & I believe
those concerned will be decorated. I'm
not sure whether the others got back, but

4.

I fancy they did. I enclose a couple of copies of the stuff I pulled off the tail. It is headed "Warning". From Great Britain to the German people". Get some one to translate it if you can — but be discreet.

The sequel to our down-flip was this :- Our intelligence learned that a large concentration of bombers was massing in Germany on the Dutch frontier. They crossed the frontier at about 3, followed by an even larger mass, bound for England. However, at about 3.30 they unaccountably turned back. I can't tell you how we knew they turned, but it is

ROYAL AIR FORCE,
TANGMERE,
CHICHESTER,
SUSSEX.

TEL. CHICHESTER 443.
TELEGRAPHIC ADDRESS, AERONAUTICS, CHICHESTER.

5.

quite interesting. So here we still are,
having not yet received our baptism
of fire, feeling rather nervy as a result,
& finding it quite hard to believe the
incredible fact that we are at war.

One must not dwell on the tragedy
that we all know this war to be. One's
mental condition is far from stable, &
varies alarmingly between
elation & depression, courage & honest-to-goodness
fear. We are all jumpy, & care must
be taken not to tread on any one's
"corns". I suppose it's the inaction &

6.

suspense. It will be better when we start.

I've sent you my Will, & my luggage has just left. The letter wont reach you for a day or two. I am informing the Bank to let you know the state of my account on your request at any time. Naturally I cant say or hint at anything about our future plans, but you will hear from me again soon.

In the meantime, much love to you all & the best of luck. We'll all need it!

Paul.

APPENDIX II
Pages from the author's logbook

YEAR 1940		AIRCRAFT		PILOT, OR 1ST PILOT	2ND PILOT, PUPIL OR PASSENGER	DUTY (INCLUDING RESULTS AND REMARKS)
MONTH	DATE	Type	No.			
—	—	—	—	—	—	— TOTALS BROUGHT FORW.
MAY	6	HURRICANE	L.1679	SELF		PATROL.
		"	"	"		VASSINCOURT-ROUVRES.
		"	"	"		RETURN.
	7	"	"	"		
	8	"	"	"		PATROL.
	10	BLITZKRIEG BEGINS.				
	"	HURRICANE	L.1679	SELF		PATROL (1 Do.215 LONG...
	"	"	"	"		"
	"	"	"	"		VASSINCOURT- BERRY
	"	"	"	"		PATROL.
	11	"	L.1679	"		PATROL (? 1 Do.17 N.E.MEZIE...
						F-LANDED MEZIERES.
	"	MUREAU	?	?	SELF	MEZIERES-BERRY
	"	HURRICANE	L.1685	SELF		PATROL.
	"	"	"	"		" (2 Me.110 BRUNEHAM...
						DOWN BY PARACHUTE RUMIGN...
	15	"	?	"		PATROL (2 Me.110 VOUZIERS
						DOWN BY PARACHUTE AMIFONTA...
	18	"	P.2805	"		VRAUX- PLEURS.
		"	P.2676	"		PATROL (A.A.St.QUENTIN
	19	"	P.2805	"		" (3 He.111 ME E.CHATEA...
						THIERRY) F-LANDED WOUNDED
						LA FERTE-SOUS-JOUARR...

GRAND TOTAL [Cols. (1) to (10)]

451 Hrs. 00 Mins.

TOTALS CARRIED FORWA...

Paul Richey's logbook and the original manuscript of *Fighter Pilot* are in the Imperial War Museum, London

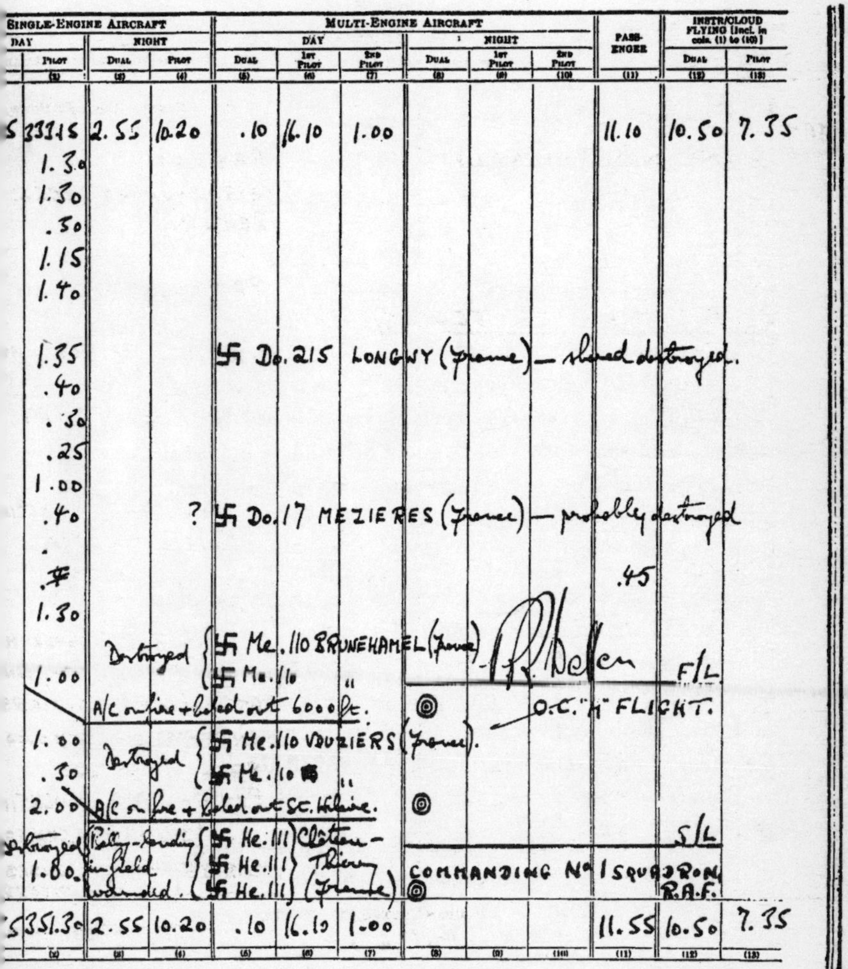

Single-Engine Aircraft			Multi-Engine Aircraft						Passenger	Instr/Cloud Flying [incl. in cols. (1) to (10)]	
Day	Night		Day			Night					
Pilot	Dual	Pilot	Dual	1st Pilot	2nd Pilot	Dual	1st Pilot	2nd Pilot		Dual	Pilot
(2)	(3)	(4)	(5)	(6)	(7)	(8)	(9)	(10)	(11)	(12)	(13)
333.15	2.55	10.20	.10	16.10	1.00				11.10	10.50	7.35
1.30											
1.30											
.50											
1.15											
1.40											
1.35			Do.215 LONGWY (France) — shared destroyed.								
.40											
.30											
.25											
1.00											
.40			? Do.17 MEZIERES (France) — probably destroyed								
.											
.#									.45		
1.30											
1.00	Destroyed		Me.110 BRUNEHAMEL (France); Me.110 " ; A/C on fire + baled out 6000 ft.			[signature] O.C. "A" FLIGHT				F/L	
1.00	Destroyed		Me.110 VOUZIERS (France); Me.110 "								
.30											
2.00			A/C on fire + baled out St. Hilaire.								
1.80	Destroyed (Belly-landing in field, wounded.)		He.111, He.111, He.111 Château-Thierry (France)			COMMANDING Nº 1 SQUADRON R.A.F.				S/L	
351.30	2.55	10.20	.10	16.10	1.00				11.55	10.50	7.35
(2)	(3)	(4)	(5)	(6)	(7)	(8)	(9)	(10)	(11)	(12)	(13)

APPENDIX III
Letter from 'Hilly' Brown

Wing Commander M. H. Brown,

Officer's Mess, R.A.F. Station,

Hawarden, Nr. Chester.   September 20 1941

Dear Paul,

I received and read your book yesterday. It was a marvellous bit of work Paul. It's veracity alone is almost unbelievable. There isn't a passage with which I might be familiar, but what I know to be true. The spirit is there too, as if you had only written when you wanted to, portraying the spirit before stopping to analyse it.

Young Baraldi showed me your picture in the *Sunday Graphic* last week, and after reading a couple of passages, I said you were undoubtedly the author. He pooh pooh'ed the idea, but I insisted, saying you were the only pilot of No.1 Sqn who would have the ability to produce a book. Sure enough, I saw Nackers on Monday, and he said he had heard all about it from Leak.

I like the way you have been so kind about the whole thing, Paul. Anyone who turned out dead-beat, was left completely out, and everyone's faults or shortcomings completely ignored.

The squadron history is now written as it should be.

Congratulations on your bar and your half-stripe, old boy. It is quite possible that we will take the air together again one day. I hope to get a wing in 11 Group soon.

Work here seems useful in a way, and we have a good lot of instructors. Nevertheless the schoolmaster feeling rears its ugly head, and I long for the comraderie (sic) of squadron life. I would gladly revert to S/L and go to form a new Squadron or back to No.1.

All the best Paul. Drop in sometime. We'll make a special effort to entertain you.

Regards,

   Hilly.

APPENDIX IV
Formation Flying

Royal Air Force fighter squadrons have always prided themselves on their formation flying, by which they practise and demonstrate the control, precision, teamwork and discipline that become operational requirements in time of war. In Fighter Command close formation was needed to allow large forces of aircraft to penetrate cloud with the minimum risk of collision or scattering. Air drill was designed primarily for this purpose, as well as for positioning sections, flights and squadrons for attack or defence, though open or 'battle' formations were used for the latter. In Vic formation, for instance, close formation required a following aircraft's wingtip to be directly astern of a leading aircraft's wingtip and ahead of its tailplane; in a good squadron this could be tightened up so that following wingtips were 'tucked in' or overlapping between a leading aircraft's wing and tailplane. Paradoxically, it was easier to keep station accurately in close formation than in open or 'battle' formation with spacing increased to 50–100 yards. Tight formation, with a few feet separating wings, tailplanes from ailerons, and propellers from wingtips or rudders, was strictly for experts. All formation flying required constant practice.

Figures 2 to 8 represent the main pre-war Fighter Command air-drill close formations, roughly in sequence of normal performance and in ascending order of difficulty. Figures 1 and 9 represent unusual small formations designed for specific purposes.

Fig 1
No 1 Squadron's famous 1937 aerobatic team of Furies performed in a tight, 'tucked in' diamond like this Hurricane formation.

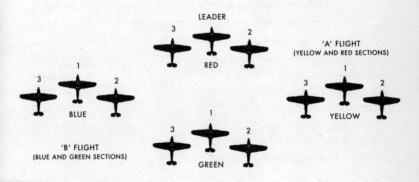

Fig 2
Squadron in Aircraft Close Vic, Sections Close Vic. Green Section is slightly below the other sections.

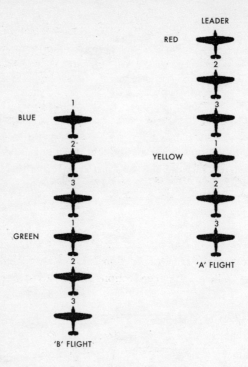

Fig 3
Squadron in Aircraft Close Line Astern, Flights Close Echelon Port.
The aircraft are slightly stepped-down astern.

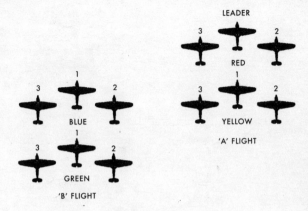

Fig 4
Squadron in Aircraft Close Vic, Sections Close Astern, Flights Close Echelon Port. Yellow and Green sections are slightly stepped-down.

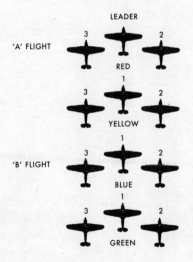

Fig 5
Squadron in Aircraft Close Vic, Sections Close Astern. The sections are slightly stepped-down astern.

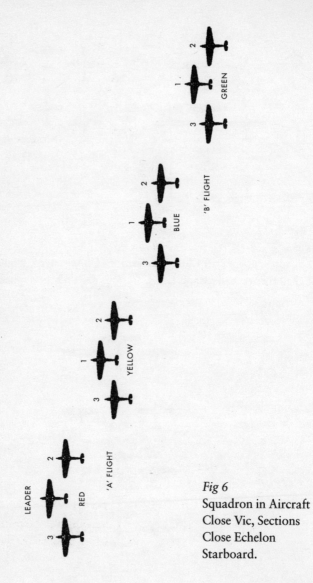

Fig 6
Squadron in Aircraft
Close Vic, Sections
Close Echelon
Starboard.

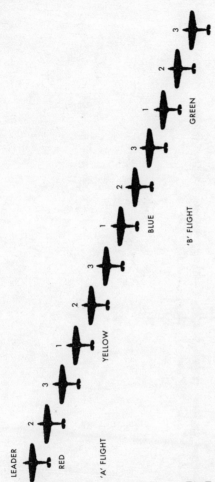

Fig 7
Squadron in Aircraft
Close Echelon Starboard.

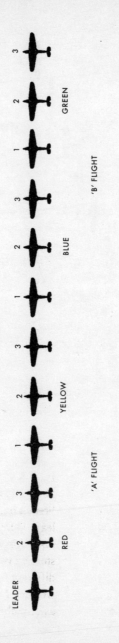

Fig 8
Squadron in Aircraft
Close Line Abreast.

50–100 yards

Fig 9
Flight of No 1 Squadron in French battle formation, as learned from the *Armée de l'Air*. Aircraft 4 and 5 are stepped well up astern at different heights and are weaving for better vision astern, above and below.

INDEX